Written

An Uncharted Life Aboard a Wooden Boat

By

Laura Mc Crossin

Scottansailor.com

Though rows are ploughed
and seeds are sown
think twice
this life's not
Written in Stone...

Anonymous

3

For
Annie Laurie

Part One

If one advances confidently in the direction of
his dreams, and endeavours to live the life
which he has imagined, he will meet with a
success unexpected in common hours.

Henry David Thoreau

One

I stood in disbelief at the end of the wooden dock in Antigua, all my worldly possessions in two bags resting at my feet. Until very recently, it was a lifestyle I had never dreamed possible.

I had been in love with tall ships for as long as I could remember. My first childhood memory was of a summer afternoon, sitting with my family in tall grass along the Dartmouth waterfront, mesmerized by the tall ships as they paraded past Georges Island and onward to the open Atlantic in 1984. When the next largest gathering of tall ships occurred years later during Tall Ships 2000, I was sure to be in attendance.

I was now twenty years old as I wandered through the crowds along the Halifax waterfront. I came upon a ship that particularly caught my eye, a hundred-and-thirty-foot square-rigged ship named *Eye of the Wind*. As I watched the crew climbing aloft, coiling lines, and taking sandpaper to the mahogany in preparation for varnishing, I wondered what kind of person you had to be to work aboard such a ship. Surely you must have spent your childhood messing around in small boats, learning important techniques and seamanship and teamwork. And you must be strong.

Myself? I was just preparing to begin my final year of a chemistry degree that saw me in the university library twelve hours daily. Not an athletic bone in my body, and never having stepped aboard a sailboat, I quickly let go of the notion of enquiring about the 'Crew Wanted' sign on the mast.

Fast forward to a year later. Having completed my chemistry degree, but with no more direction in life or thoughts of what I could do with this degree, I began some serious soul-searching. I decided a week with my own thoughts at Kejimkujik National Park might somehow help, so I packed my tent and sleeping bag and made the ninety-minute drive. I eventually set up camp beside Jeremy Lake and began to write. Aside from the occasional hiker passing through the collection of campsites, I was on my own.

I thought long and hard about what had brought me to that moment. With so much to be explored in this world and so many ways for time to be spent, what had kept me in that dismal, miserable library for the last three years, studying material that didn't interest me, in preparation for a career choice I hadn't questioned since childhood? Why did I want to become a veterinarian or a doctor? The time spent alone didn't answer those questions, but instead I realized I'd been asking the wrong questions to begin with. I instead decided to ponder *if*, not *why*, either one of those things were what I wanted, and by the end of the week, the answer was an emphatic *no*.

It was a liberating self-discovery, but implicitly terrifying. What would I do now? Academia was all I had ever known, and now tomorrow, next month, in fact, the *rest of my life* was a complete unknown. I'd known many who would go on to become professional students, some in an attempt to avoid what I was feeling in this moment; to postpone that step into real life, and to continue living in the safety of a predetermined schedule. Following that road seemed more terrifying to me than the unknown, like stepping aboard an express train in youth, only to watch in agony as everything worth taking in went hurtling past, eventually learning there would be no stops until retirement.

I had to make a decision about *something. Anything.* I didn't know what I would do next with my life, but at the very least, I knew it was time to return the car I had borrowed from my parents a week earlier.

On my way back to Halifax, as an afterthought and never expecting anything to come of it, I veered onto the ramp for Exit Eleven, which would take me to Lunenburg. I had visited the town frequently over the years with my family during Sunday drives from the city. It was often heavy with fog and the smell of tarred docks and salt air, with the ghostly sound of the foghorn coming from the breakwater. Colourful historic houses and shops adorn the hillside that sweeps down into the harbour, where dozens of boats lay safely at anchor. Whenever I paid a visit to Lunenburg, I never wanted to leave.

After wandering the streets for a while, I took a walk down to the famous *Bluenose II*, the successor to *Bluenose*, the ship on the Canadian dime. As an ambassador for the province of Nova Scotia, each year they took on a crew of twelve deckhands, many without previous sailing experience. This was news to me. Learning this fact from a deckhand that afternoon suddenly opened a whole other world of opportunity.

Unfortunately, it was much too late to apply that season. As I turned to walk down the wharf, Julie called out. She had suddenly remembered another boat just half a mile down the road. The boat was out of the water in a local shipyard for *refit*, meaning she was having a thorough overhaul, having been built entirely of wood in 1924. They needed general labourers: anyone willing to paint, sand, varnish, or anything else in need of doing. She was to set sail in a month, and perhaps this would be a foot in the door.

I'll admit there was much hesitation on my part as I walked down the docks. What would I say to the

Captain? I was extremely shy and introverted, not to mention I had absolutely no experience. Sailing was something I had never seriously considered or ever dreamed I was capable of doing. How could I exude confidence and enthusiasm about a world I knew nothing about?

When I rounded the bend in the road the ship came into sight, an original Grand Banks schooner not much different from *Bluenose* herself. I was in love. Her name was *Highlander Sea*. I nervously climbed the two flights of steps to reach the deck of the ship. Finding no one on deck, I found a hatch and climbed below, totally oblivious to the customary *permission to board* etiquette. Once below, I was face to face with the Captain, an attractive and intimidating young man whose stern glare I interpreted as insult at finding a stranger aboard. I quickly blurted out my best explanation, and, before taking the time to consider what I might be getting myself into, I stated that this was something I felt I *had* to do. In turn, he told me about the vessel, and explained that she was the flagship of a Dartmouth company which ran offshore supply vessels, and, officially, all potential crew had to submit resumes to the main office for consideration. Being impatient, I was unhappy with any response that would delay my pursuit of this newfound passion. Still, I could hardly contain my excitement during the drive back to Dartmouth.

Upon finding the offices on the Dartmouth waterfront, I offered my resume to the secretary. Without looking up, and still typing with one hand, she reached up with the other and tossed my resume amidst a pile of strewn papers at the end of the desk, likely never to be seen again. I asked if those were other resumes for *Highlander Sea*. Chomping her gum and motioning with her hand, she informed me the stack of resumes for *Highlander* was *this high*, and that mine would be going at the *bottom*.

Obviously, I was getting nowhere. I went back out to the car, heart in my stomach, severely disappointed. Just one hour earlier I had felt my life was about to change drastically; I had seen a whole new possibility for an adventurous life I had previously believed could only belong to others. I couldn't let this go. I started the car, resolving to return to Lunenburg that afternoon to prove to the Captain I was serious.

Upon finding the Captain, I explained how I hadn't been taken seriously at the office, and this was an opportunity I did not want to miss. I would start work now, and would work for free. I handed him my resume, as if to make it official.

"You drove all the way back down here today just to tell me that?" he asked, grinning, impressed at my determination I hoped. Giving me the benefit of the doubt, he shook my hand and said, "You're hired."

§§§

With an impossible amount of work to accomplish, but the right mix of crew for the job, the boat was re-launched on schedule, and I'd earned my position aboard for the summer. We were to take part in the Tall Ships events taking place in the Great Lakes, and departing Halifax in late June with a crew of sixteen, I experienced the open ocean for the first time in my life.

Awoken for the midnight-to-four watch, we felt the icy mist pour over the ship and into our bones, as the southeast wind rolled over still-frigid waters. Looking over the side, I saw glowing green streaks, and had somehow until now been oblivious to the existence of phosphorescence, a phenomenon created primarily by dinoflagellate plankton, which respond when the water is disturbed by emitting a brief, luminous glow. It was pure magic to this til-now landlubber.

Another week at sea, sailing up the St Lawrence Seaway, found us in Québec City. Shortly thereafter, many of us experienced the locks of the seaway for the first time, which our elementary school text books described as near fables, that by simply controlling water levels, they could allow massive ocean-going tankers as far west as Lake Superior. We were able to learn first-hand how it was done.

We won many of the Tall Ship races that

season, losing only occasionally to Maryland's *Pride of Baltimore II.* We worked long hours, even at the dock. Our invitations to the host cities required us to open our decks for others to have a glimpse of how we lived. Often, we would remain closed in the mornings for necessary maintenance before opening to the public, and we would take turns extending our workdays to cover the essential 24-hour watch system. This was necessary for security, not only for the few times strangers attempted to board (usually on a late-night dare when wandering home from the pub), but also to keep watch over the boat in general; to ensure that we weren't dragging anchor, to check that dock lines were secure, or to watch that our generators did not overheat.

Two months flew by quickly and by September 11th, the evening watch team was a clump of chattering teeth as we sailed off the coast of Québec's Gaspé Peninsula. Not until the bosun emerged from below decks, having received a call from his wife on the satellite phone, did we have any hint of how the world had changed that morning.

We made our way back to Halifax, and when not speculating on the details surrounding the collapse of the twin towers, talk was around the upcoming winter season, and who would be lucky enough to escape south aboard another ship. I hadn't expected or desired to be one of them. I was exhausted from a summer of non-stop activity, night shifts, and rough weather. At this point, I had the feeling this sailing thing had run its course.

I had caught the bug though, and only one week after leaving *Highlander,* I ached for the sea once more. With my foot in the door, and being reliable and having a strong work ethic, one opportunity led to another. Over the next year, I jumped from one ship to another, travelling from Nova Scotia to the eastern United States, eventually finding myself Caribbean bound. At this point in my life, free and single and no debts or responsibilities back home, it was by far the best way to travel. Most ships took care of food and board, and normally paid a small weekly stipend to allow enjoyment of the odd night ashore.

Upon arrival in the British Virgin Islands, I was required to leave my current boat, *Bonnie Lynn*, as they had charter guests arriving and really had only been doing me a favour by permitting me to take part in the passage. Looking back on it now, I sometimes wonder how I had the nerve to travel in this manner. As I joined each ship, it was always for an indeterminate amount of time, and I didn't always know where I was going to end up. I never knew once my time was up on one vessel, if there would necessarily be another ship willing to take me on. The captain of *Bonnie Lynn* kindly asked around the anchorage if anyone was willing to take a volunteer crew to Antigua, where my research had informed me that a tall ship, *Stad*

Amsterdam, would be attending the yacht broker show. I was absolutely determined to angle my way into a position aboard this ship.

I arrived early on a December morning in Falmouth Harbour, Antigua aboard a small boat named *Too Elusive*. I quickly eyed the docks for the traditional, square-rigged masts I had come in search of. To my surprise, there were two such ships meeting those criteria. Upon rowing ashore, I discovered that one was indeed *Stad Amsterdam*. The other? *Eye of the Wind*.

Suddenly my desires had changed drastically. *Stad Amsterdam* had beckoned me there, but *Eye of the Wind* is where I knew I belonged. I approached Captain Svend, this time exuding confidence and enthusiasm, arrogantly convinced I would be hired on the spot. It was fate, after all. My heart sank as he explained they simply were not in need of any new crew, nor did they even have a spare bunk. But persistence had gotten me aboard *Highlander*, so I wasn't about to let this dream slip through my fingers just yet.

Eye of the Wind was scheduled to be in port another six days, and I told Svend that I was willing to volunteer for the next few days, just for the experience.

"Okay, but, I really cannot pay you anything…"

Over the next week, I became intimately acquainted with the ships plaque, an approximately 200 square-inch hunk of brass that likely hadn't seen Brasso since it was cast in 1912. Eight hours a day I would sit on the ships hatch, with Brasso-soaked and blackened rags. Svend would walk by, laughing and shaking his head, reminding me there were no available bunks, but I was welcome to have lunch and dinner aboard with the crew for the remainder of the week. On the morning of day six, Svend summoned me to the aft deck, shook my hand, and welcomed me aboard. It turned out there *had* been a spare bunk all along, though it still remained true that the ship was not in need of additional crew. My persistence had persuaded him to not leave me behind.

So here I was on an Antiguan dock, having gathered the last of my belongings from *Too Elusive*, preparing to step aboard the tall ship that would be my home for the foreseeable future. My first day as hired crew, shining yet more brass, helping to load provisions, then climbing to the top of the mast to unfurl the sails as we prepared to sail to St Martin, my thoughts drifted back to Tall Ships 2000. It struck me how everything had come full circle, and I had become one of *those* people, living a life few imagine possible for themselves, and was now on the inside looking out.

Two

I would spend close to nine months aboard *The Eye,* as those aboard affectionately called her. We sailed throughout the Windward Islands, from St Martin to Grenada and back again. The owner of the ship had ultimately planned a circumnavigation, with the Galapagos being the next destination after a Caribbean tour. Plans changed though, as they often do. In March, the Captain informed us we were bound on a trans-Atlantic, and in six weeks, would be in his homeport of Copenhagen, Denmark. We left St. Martin one final time in early April, and made the eight-day sail to our first stop, Bermuda.

Despite staying at anchor for close to a week in St George's Harbour, few things stick out in my mind as clearly as the afternoon I spent alone in an old cemetery near the west end of the island. Many of the stones marked the graves of young sailors, as far back as the late 1700's. I remember the detail of some of the stones, how descriptive they sometimes were of the circumstances surrounding a death. One sailor, eighteen years old, had fallen to his death from the topgallant yard of a square-rigged vessel over a hundred years earlier. He hit the starboard deck and was killed instantly. I've always been drawn to graveyards by their natural solemnity. They're an authoritative reminder of how temporary everything is in this life, while reinforcing the futility of sweating the small stuff.

After loading provisions, which included cases of the local Goslings Black Seal rum, we were bound for the Azores, two weeks to our east. Most days were like the one before, apart from a small collection of defining moments.

The first of these moments was our near miss at dawn of a large container, which had fallen off a cargo ship. The two thousand cubic foot steel container periodically disappeared below the surface with the passing swells, barely visibly until almost adjacent to the helmsmen. We were sailing along at nine knots[1], and had our course been a few meters to the right, we likely would have found ourselves abandoning ship and taking to the life rafts.

The second memorable morning began when those of us off watch were roused from our bunks by the panicked voice of another deckhand, shouting the

---

[1] A unit of speed, equaling one nautical mile per hour, approximately 1.2 mph.

words no sailor wants to hear in such a tone, "*All hands on deck!*" We were under close-to-full sail when we suddenly found ourselves surrounded by a series of waterspouts.[2] Like tornadoes, waterspouts can move along unpredictable paths. Many advise to continue along a straight course, rather than trying to steer around one that could possibly turn ninety degrees without warning. In such circumstances, it's against human nature to stand there and essentially do nothing, so Svend chose to zigzag around them. Right or wrong, we managed to avoid all of them, and afterwards were wishing someone had taken the opportunity to grab a camera.

Svend had a very Danish way of speaking English, precise and with absolute clarity. "Oh Laura, you are but a weak woman!" he used to tease, as he often picked up on my need to prove I could do everything the boys could do. This really wasn't necessary aboard *The Eye*, though, as it had been on other ships. We were all very much a family on board. Perhaps it was Svend's fatherly characteristics, wanting his 'children' to be the best they could be, or perhaps it was because his wife, essentially the First Mate, was aboard. Whatever the reason, female crew were treated as equals, and that brings me to the third defining moment.

It was a cold sunny evening, one day before our

---

[2]Simply defined as tornadoes over the water

expected landfall in the Azores, and at the tail end of a gale whose winds were blowing off Newfoundland's Grand Banks. In twenty-five foot seas, myself and my friend Katie were sent aloft to the top-gallant yard, as high as one can go aboard *The Eye*, to tie down sails that had become loose in the powerful wind. Once the task was complete, we stayed a moment to take it all in; beluga whales visible just beneath the surface below, playful dolphins doing barrel-rolls out of the sides of the waves, and in every direction were mountainous swells, beyond which I thought I caught a glimpse of eternity.

Arriving in the Azores early morning, we sailed into the lee of the island of Faial, the seas subsided, and many of us had our first glimpse of these remote mid-Atlantic Islands. In Horta, one of the main safe harbours within the island archipelago, we were introduced to the famous Peter's Café Sport, and were immediately captivated by the wallpaper. Literally hundreds of small letters, simply addressed by boat names, adorned the walls of the quaint café. The café offered itself as a sort of central post office for sailors. If you had friends who'd be arriving at a later date aboard another vessel, you could leave your message tacked to the wall and hope they would find it upon arrival. I wondered at the time how many of the letters had been there for years, left for friends who would never reach their destination. As we really weren't travelling in the company of other boats, we decided to leave a letter behind for the next *Eye of the Wind* crew, whenever the ship might visit there again. As we shared a few twenty-five cent pints, we passed around a sheet of paper, each taking the time to write a few lines of wisdom. All these years later, *The Eye* has not made a stop in Horta since. Our letter will still be on that wall, growing brown and brittle.

Two more weeks found us alongside in Copenhagen. I recall sharing a common sentiment with many of my shipmates at the end of our crossing. None of us felt we had just sailed across the Atlantic. I'm not sure how I expected to feel when it was over, but it certainly didn't seem like any grand accomplishment that one might imagine it would be when dreaming of future adventures as a child. It was just a series of day sails, each day beginning a little further down the line. The fact that sailing across the Atlantic hadn't seemed overly difficult led me to believe that a multitude of other things in life I once perceived as beyond my reach were probably no such thing.

After that crossing, I felt I could do anything.

§§§

All good things must come to an end sometime, and shortly after arriving in Denmark, it was time to leave *Eye of the Wind*. I was closer to my ancestral home of Scotland than I had ever been, and weary of sailing life for the moment. I packed my backpack and committed myself to spending a month travelling throughout Scotland.

Three weeks in, I remember looking out the window of the train as I approached *The Gateway to the Highlands*, Stirling. Gentle sloped hills to the south paired with towering mountains to the north created an extraordinary backdrop. Stirling Castle sat atop a volcanic outcrop between the two, from which the rest of the town trickled down. It was a feeling of coming home like I'd never felt before. I decided that day I would move to Stirling for a while. After settling in to my first flat, I called home to tell my family I had left the ship, and I went on to describe where I was living.

"Stirling? That's where your ancestors lived before boarding their ship for Canada in 1832," my mother informed me. I felt like the memories and longings of that young couple who had left Stirling so long ago for the New World had survived and been passed through the generations; feelings that would lay dormant, only to resurface when a distant descendant was finally able to lay eyes upon their home turf once more. I imagined how difficult it must have been to tear themselves away from this beautiful country, the only place they had ever known, knowing they would never be coming home.

What was originally intended to be a one-month

stay turned into fourteen. I secured a position at a local coffee shop, and joined a local pipe band, having been an avid bagpiper since age eleven. Over the next year with the Royal Burgh of Stirling Pipes and Drums, I travelled throughout Scotland and Ireland for highland gatherings, including the British, European, and finally the World Championships in Glasgow, and even joined them for a performance in Paris. We rehearsed a lot, but never too seriously, and accordingly we all had a fabulous time and never placed in the top ten of a single competition. We had frequent performances in the courtyard of Stirling Castle, a popular location for American businesses to hold conventions, and they would get everything they expected to find in Scotland: men in skirts and feather bonnets, playing Scotland the Brave and Amazing Grace, followed by a banquet of haggis, neeps, tatties, and mushy peas.

I don't recall a single dull moment during those fourteen months. Nevertheless, something was missing, and I decided it was the sea, and Nova Scotia. There was nothing left to do but go home.

Three

Arriving home in Halifax in late summer, I enrolled in a one-year program to study meteorology, for the sake of something to do. I was no longer happy working in coffee shops, and meteorology was something that had captured my interest since childhood. The job prospects upon completing the degree were excellent, and I thought perhaps by taking a job for a year or two in my hometown I might become more centered on where I wanted the rest of my life to lead, and perhaps even meet someone.

While working toward my degree, I applied for a deckhand position aboard *Bluenose II,* assuming I might not find a forecasting job immediately upon graduation. Now having four years of on-and-off experience aboard ships, I thought it would be a fitting finale to my tall ship career before the inevitable entry into the 'real world'. It was yet another dream that was to come true. It was a magnificent summer aboard, sailing throughout Nova Scotia, New Brunswick, and New England. It was incredible to witness, first-hand, the special place the ship had in so many Canadians hearts, and how their faces would beam when they were simply permitted to walk her decks.

As the days grew shorter and the sailing season drew to an end, we gradually dismantled the boat for her winter sleep. Three days after signing off the ship, I received a phone call from a Halifax company who had kept my resume on file. As a company who offered wind and sea state forecasts for Nova Scotia's offshore oil and natural gas industry, they were impressed with my maritime background and invited me in for an interview, and soon thereafter, my career began.

It was the first job I had received based on my university education, and I was pleased with my new salary, having lived primarily off minimum wage, and often much less, for the last five years. It was a freedom I had longed for, after many years in close quarters with shipmates, sleeping in bunks half the size of a single bed, and living the strict schedule required for the efficient running of ships. Now, I had a place of my own, in my hometown which I had always loved so much. Working longer days in exchange for more days off in between, I felt, for a very short while, that I had it made.

I always thought Halifax had a lot to offer. I was able to go to a wonderful yoga loft on a regular basis, and, as an insomniac, was grateful for the 24-hour coffee shop on the waterfront. I would spend hours there, writing in my journal, reading local newspapers, and secretly hoping to meet someone. I always relished that hopeful feeling as a chronically single woman, imagining the romantic possibilities that could lie ahead with a surprise encounter.

Working alone, though, for twelve hours a day, and returning home to an empty apartment on a quiet street, I fell into the same trap so many do. It became a challenge to reconnect with old friends who had continued to sail, and I had long since lost touch with many of my friends from high school and university who had moved on to jobs or graduate programs, mostly in other provinces. I had too much time on my hands to think about everything I had been through until now. I was beginning to miss all the interesting characters I had met over the years. It's a difficult conundrum to accept, that you would never have met so many of the incredible characters who have come into your life if it weren't for your free spirit, the same free spirit that guarantees you will not be with those people for long.

I could no longer see my future in a context of optimism. What I *could* see of it depressed me. I had fallen into the nine-to-five trap, and after years of adventure, I felt a horrible unrest. Was this *it*? Was my adventure over and it was time to settle down? No one was forcing me to accept any of this, but my situation bred lethargy, and lethargy controlled my situation. It seemed easier to stay miserable in this existence than to concoct another plan of what to do next. I had forgotten the lessons I had learned in my early days of sailing, that all that's really required is to take that first courageous step, with direction and intent, and the world will conspire to help you. But as it is a disease of my generation, with too many options and rampant indecision, I simply didn't know what I wanted to do next. I only knew I was unhappy with where I was now.

One Saturday morning, after pumping liquid soap onto my toothbrush, then shuffling to the kitchen to find the milk in the cupboard, I knew something had to be done to turn off the automatic pilot that had assumed control of my existence. I had to rediscover my passion for living. Ultimately, it became a matter of circumstance that weekend rather than an active search for something extreme that knocked the train off its tracks and set my life back on its proper course. Close friends had their wooden schooner in a local yacht club, and always welcomed extra hands in preparing for the upcoming sailing season. In exchange for good company and rum, I jumped on my bicycle and headed over to help.

After a few hours work, we sat back for a break, and surveyed our surroundings. A few slips over sat a small, two-masted wooden boat named *Rissa*. My friends heard a rumour she was for sale. A broad, stoutly-built royal blue hull, tall spruce masts, and a reaching bowsprit that made her appear twice the size, I walked over to the other pier for a closer look. Peering through the windows, I could see she had everything I would need: a kerosene cook-stove, cabin heater, icebox, a couple of bunks, and a small washroom. And she was surprisingly spacious. Anne-Louise stood beside me, encouraging the stars in my eyes, commenting how she'd be a 'great first boat' for me. Not that I was in the market for a boat. Or was I?

Rissa was a Rosborough design. The Rosborough family were a fourth-generation Nova Scotian boat building family, and, as I would discover much later, this little boat would be their final hull built of wood. Commissioned by a Polish gentleman in 1986, he abandoned the project mid-construction. The remainder of the task fell to one of the Rosborough sons, and in 1991, she was finally launched as *Molly*. She was eventually sold to a fellow named Terry, who gave her the name *Rissa*. He was her latest owner, and someone I would unfortunately never have the pleasure of meeting.

Terry's story was heartbreaking. *Rissa* had been a beautiful sight as she sat on her mooring in the small cove beside their waterfront home. Approaching retirement from his position at a Halifax museum, Terry had plans for taking *Rissa* south to the Bahamas for many winters to come, while returning each summer to his Nova Scotia home. As the story was related to me, he had postponed retirement for a couple of years, hoping to put the extra money earned towards home repairs and preparing *Rissa* for sea. Each year he contemplated his journey, and each year, there was another reason to stay with his job a while longer. When Terry finally retired, with plans of sailing south the following autumn, he was shortly thereafter diagnosed with cancer. He died in September.

It was a difficult three months, both in negotiating with his widow, and procuring a loan. She was understandably emotional over the sale, and the banks were understandably wary of loaning money to a young woman in a new career, with collateral that could set sail for foreign ports at any time. I received rejection after rejection, until I encountered that one person, Goran, willing to go the extra mile to make the loan possible.

Papers signed, it was now time to collect my new boat, and my new home. My friend, whom I call Super Dave, came along to help. A past captain of mine from a ship I'd joined for a short stint to Gloucester, Massachusetts, his sailing and engineering skills I knew and trusted. Without him on board that day, I would have planted *Rissa* square on James' Rock, just moments after taking ownership and leaving the dock. I was unprepared: no charts, no idea how to get out of Purcell's Cove, no radar, and in the thick of fog. Dave recognized the tell-tale signs of shallow rocks by the seaweed that was licking the surface dead ahead. I'm forever grateful that he was aboard that day.

Acquiring the boat and my last available days in the apartment before my sub-letters arrived didn't exactly coincide, and I was homeless for eight days. I can't tell you where I slept that week, but I will tell you that all my belongings had to be stored somewhere, and the forecasting company kindly offered the spare office on a short-term basis. As I walked through the pedway, with pillows and a backpack and a pair of Helly Hanson sailing boots, a strangers voice called out behind me.

"Those look like sailors boots, you must be a sailor."

His name was Peter, an investments adviser, ex-Navy Captain and life-long sailor. Unalterably personable, it wasn't difficult to keep a conversation going with him, and within a few minutes, he knew my entire story. He seemed to sense before I did the difficulties I was destined to encounter. He gave me his business card, and told me not to hesitate to call if there was any way he could be of assistance. It wouldn't be long before I took him up on the offer.

I was now a full-time live-aboard, which was difficult to accomplish within city limits. No yacht club would knowingly accept a boat into their fleet with a full-time live-aboard, and any city dock was generally for overnight stays, or otherwise short term rental, and in my books, unaffordable. My whole grand scheme in affording my new lifestyle was to avoid paying rent in order to make the monthly loan payments. I would have to be creative if I wanted to make this work.

As I bounced around from dock to dock throughout that first summer, I came into contact with thousands of locals and tourists who were drawn to my miniature tall ship. Many found it hard to believe that a young, single woman was up to the task of handling this boat on her own. I thought of Svend a lot, *you are only a weak woman!* But I knew his comment was always in jest. Some folks had passing rhetorical questions like *Daddy's yacht, huh?* Others shook their heads with a sceptical look and tone of disbelief, *Good luck lady*! Most though, from my recollection, seemed to wish they had thought of the idea themselves.

Much to my own embarrassment on a number of occasions, when approaching the dock beside a popular waterfront restaurant, I would miss my mark, and either gently crash into the dock, or end up too far away from the wharf to tie a dock line. It was the only way I knew how to learn, so I would try to imagine there weren't dozens of people seated at that fine seafood restaurant, and that I was invisible to those wandering the docks, enjoying their cones of *Cow's* ice cream. When my imagination wasn't enough, and perhaps this doesn't help the plight of women who are trying to overcome similar hurdles, but I always felt better loudly announcing my excuse *I'm just a girl!* whenever I drew attention to myself by crunching into a wharf.

As I became more accustomed to manoeuvring my new boat alone, one of my favourite perks of my new existence on Halifax waters was McNabbs Island. Situated at the mouth of the harbour, and with only a handful of inhabitants, it was an oasis from the hustle and bustle of city life. I would stock up my icebox with ice, good food, and wine, and I'd sail over to the pier just north of Maughers Beach (also known as Hangman's Beach because of its use by the Royal Navy to hang the bodies of executed mutineers as a warning to crews of ships entering the harbour to stay on their best behaviour). I would wander through what remained of the forts, a cemetery containing some of the island's earliest residents, and the burial site of cholera victims from the *S. S. England*. I walked the rocky beaches and collected the more obscure items that would wash ashore. The strangest was a coconut, from who knows where, whose weathered appearance led me to believe it was quite plausible that it had made its entire journey from the tropics to Nova Scotia by sea.

Slowly, I learned how to handle my new vessel and a few weeks later it was time to make my first voyage outside the harbour.

Four

I recall vividly my first passage from Halifax to Lunenburg with *Rissa,* now renamed *Annie Laurie,* for the song written by a Scottish soldier long ago, as a proclamation of his love for his sweetheart back home. We set out on a Friday morning in August, with an intended destination of Second Peninsula near Lunenburg. The re-launching of the fully rebuilt *Valkyrie*, a twenty-nine foot wooden sloop originally built and launched on that same beach at Second Peninsula in 1946, was taking place Saturday on the afternoon tide. The work was completed by a professional boat builder in Halifax whom I had become acquainted with a month earlier when he recognized *Annie Laurie* as having previously belonged to his friend and co-worker, Terry. The launching was also to be a memorial for Terry, his widow would be there, and I was asked if I would bring the boat down for the event.

Wanting to get an early start, I planned a

departure of 7:00 AM. Having owned the boat for less than a month, I was still becoming acquainted with her systems, and I shouldn't have been shocked when the engine wouldn't start immediately. The batteries were dead (what did I know about properly maintaining 12-volt batteries at the time?) I didn't know what to do to remedy this situation quickly, and I did feel rushed, it being nearly sixty miles we had to make that day, for a boat that could average little more than four knots. I called my friend Super Dave once again. While in Nova Scotia, he was always the first person that would come to mind when I needed help with anything boat-related, and he never let me down.

The invitation to Second Peninsula forced me to cram many things I had been avoiding, and a quick radio check with the VHF confirmed that I was able to receive, but not transmit, on the radio. It is law, but more importantly it's common sense not to leave port without a working radio, in case of an emergency. By 10:00 AM, Dave had the engine going and the batteries charging, and had scrounged-up a spare hand-held VHF to take along. We were off to the races. Well, we would have been, if there had been a breath of wind. Nevertheless, thanks to the 'iron jib' (a Perkins 4-108 diesel engine) we didn't have to wait for wind nor tide.

I will now introduce my original crew, consisting of two sailors and a wooden boat builder. My sister Katie was up for the weekend excursion, and

I knew with her would come chocolate and great breakfasts. And I was thrilled when my friend Colin offered to help, giving up his coveted one day off every two weeks from sailing *Bluenose II*. Colin is also a very talented artist in the field of film and photography, and I'm grateful for the record of memories he created with our cameras on that trip, providing me with photos and footage of the early days, which I might not have made the effort to record on my own. Lastly, a visiting boat builder offering a course at the Maritime Museum of the Atlantic was looking to increase his sailing experience on wooden boats, rather than just assembling them. I happily agreed, thinking if I encountered any sort of major leak, Wyatt would be just the man to have aboard.

We motored out of Halifax Harbour, and it appeared the fog would continue retreating from the coast. It didn't take Katie long to notice that the co-ordinates on my archaic hand-held GPS hadn't changed since we'd left the dock. Not knowing how to reset it, it was utterly useless. I saw this as an opportunity to finally test everything I had learned over the years on various tall ships. It was suddenly more urgent though when it was my own boat at stake. I instantly longed for the days of working on other boats, where the ultimate responsibility and worry belonged to someone else. Through all the learning that took place on other ships, I always knew that the Officer of the Watch had the ultimate responsibility, and was double-checking every plot the trainee deckhands made on the chart. Now, I had no such reassurance. Without a GPS, I was relying solely on my compass and paper charts, taking sights of three known points of land and plotting our position as where the three lines coincided. I was pleased with myself as we progressed, and my plots became increasingly accurate (accuracy can be gauged by how small the resulting triangle that's formed by the three lines. If your third line falls directly over the 'X' of the first two, then you have a very accurate position).

It was about 1:00 PM when we spotted the famous Nova Scotia landmark, Peggy's Cove Lighthouse. It is a very distinct sight, absolutely unmistakable to any native Nova Scotian, as it is represented on everything from place-mats to postcards, dishtowels to Christmas ornaments, and is a popular destination for Sunday drives any time of the year.

Most Maritimers know the expression, 'If you don't like the weather, just wait a minute…' and not that any of us were complaining, but moments after taking a final sight of Peggy's Cove, mist and fog began to roll in, and visibility quickly diminished to a varying ½ to 1 nautical mile. Now I wished I had that GPS. I was left with the most basic of navigational techniques, dead reckoning. For the next ten hours we would try our best to keep on our compass course, while watching how fast the water passed the hull so we could make an estimate of our speed through the water.

I went below to take another look at the chart and to make an estimate of our current location. I gave Colin a new compass course to account for the shift in the wind direction that accompanied the fog. The wind had increased, and we were finally able to sail. That was reassuring, because without radar, it's hard to know if you're about to hit another boat in the fog if you can't have some sort of audio clues, which the sound of the engine can easily disguise. What if another boat had been on a collision course, and was also quietly under sail without radar or a foghorn? We all tried not to think about that.

At some point that afternoon, I decided to change our destination to Lunenburg. I had sailed in and out of there many times on other boats, and it had a well-marked harbour and channel. Foghorns and bell buoys would be there to guide us in, though I really was banking on the fog lifting well before our arrival. Second Peninsula was obscure to me at the time, with small day-markers that weren't lit, let alone fitted with any kind of sound signals. I had never been there before, and I didn't want my first time to be a midnight arrival in the fog.

As the hours passed, I made educated guesses every fifteen minutes as to where I thought we were, and I plotted those guesses on the chart. At around four in the afternoon, visibility temporarily improved to about two miles, and I was confident that we'd soon see either Big Duck or Little Duck Island off our starboard side, and it wouldn't be long to Lunenburg. Instead, Colin spotted a red and green bell buoy. That was completely unexpected; according to my charts, there were no such buoys for miles in any direction of my assumed position. I asked him to sail closer so we could read its identifying numbers. Disbelief soon followed, as we realized we were at the approaches of Shag Harbour. We had yet to even reach Peggy's Cove.

An absolutely unmistakable sight to every Nova Scotian.

Then what was that vision of the lighthouse on the rocks that had fooled all of us? It turned out we had spotted the lighthouse on Betty's Island. *I won't make that mistake again*, was all I could tell myself, as I tried not to lose my focus on the big task that still lay ahead. The fog closed in around us once more. The southeasterly swells were increasing and the ride was becoming less comfortable. We were many, many miles from where I wanted to be, and darkness wouldn't be long coming.

I took a deep breath, tried not to let my confidence take too hard of a knock, and I recalculated the rest of our course based on our newfound position. I came to a decision, and told Colin the plan. We would sail a northwesterly course for X amount of time, then we would have to change our course and sail a southwesterly course for another hour, and if visibility remained what it was, Cross Island, at the mouth of Lunenburg Bay, would magically appear out of the fog. I couldn't believe my luck when, plus or minus fifteen minutes of when I predicted, Cross Island lay before us. It was 10:00 PM, and our final course change to aim for the inner harbour had us on a beautifully calm run dead down wind. The remainder of the fog lifted, and we all breathed sighs of relief. We were going to make last call at The Knot.

Awakening under blue skies and gentle breezes, we backtracked to Second Peninsula, approached the beach and anchored amongst the multitude of other wooden boats. The launch was a moving sight; a classic boat with a renewed soul, being given a second chance at life. I hoped Terry's wife thought similarly about *Rissa,* and may have gained a sort of comfort in seeing her sailing once again.

§§§

A year would pass, and in the meantime I would learn a lesson on how careful one must be when hiring a marine surveyor.

It was late March, and I was motoring out of Halifax Harbour before sunrise, masts lashed to the deck, as I'd taken them out for storage and refinishing before winter. With frost on the cabin top, I was dancing a jig despite full winter garb, trying to keep warm. I was Lunenburg-bound to begin repairs on the extensive rot I had discovered over the winter in her bow. I was determined to get this major work out of the way and get an early start on the sailing season.

For the work to be done, she had to be hauled out of the water. I had been so anxious to get her to Lunenburg to get the work started, I hadn't even considered that the tides might not be sufficiently "full" enough to float her onto the cradle of the marine railway[3]. "Hurry up and wait" the shipwright would say. One week and a dozen attempts later, she was finally on the cradle, and we were able to slide her up the tracks to dry land.

There was always something to be accomplished while waiting for the tides or the weather. Inside the neighbouring Dory Shop, I was able to carve my name board and refinish my masts and booms on rainy days by the warmth of the wood stove.

I would have been harbouring regrets if I had not had the ambition to get the repairs done sooner rather than later, as daydreams of a possible journey south began to take shape. I learned a great deal about her construction through the process of her

---

[3] Tracks that extend into the water so a boat can be hauled up on a cradle for maintenance or repairs.

deconstruction, as the shipwright and I hacked away at her rotten bow. Over the following months the restoration ensued; the new stem (the backbone of a ships bow) we built of oak originally intended for Pictou's tall ship *Hector*, and a length of Angelique imported from South America comprised the fifteen new planks that were needed to make her whole. The shipwright assured me I could T-bone any dock in the harbour and come out relatively unscathed, though I aim to never test that theory.

Those days were long and hard, and sometimes frustrating when things didn't go as planned. I will admit I was sometimes reduced to tears when I looked at her, bow-less and mast-less, and hundreds of hours of hard work ahead. But now, with all that behind, I was able to consider other options for the future. Having already experienced one winter aboard, and with the next winter fast approaching, and still single and feeling wholly unfulfilled in my work, there wasn't a whole lot keeping me in Halifax. I continued to carry Terry's story with me, a warning not to let life slip by unnoticed. His circumstances instilled a fear in me, a feeling of urgency; anything could happen to any one of us at any time, so I couldn't justify putting off my dreams, no matter how premature they may have seemed, until it was too late. Besides, I lived in a mobile home. I could take her almost anywhere. Why put up with another bitterly cold winter when the possibility of warm tropical waters awaited?

So, on September 8th, a little over one year after she became mine, I resolved to embark on my first major journey aboard *Annie Laurie.*

I had a short timeframe to make the trip happen that year. Weather-wise, all experienced sailors are aware of the June to November hurricane season, during which time it's best to cruise further north, in Canada's Atlantic provinces and the northeastern United States, where the cooler water temperatures are rarely able to sustain the life of a hurricane, should it happen to track in this direction from its southern origin. After November 1st, the risk of hurricane formation becomes minimal, and discomfort of living aboard in Nova Scotia begins a steady incline.

I had no desire to re-live the horrors of another winter at the dock in Dartmouth. Masts out and the boat under a blue tarpaulin, *Annie Laurie* was alongside and subject to blasting northerlies funnelling down the Narrows of Halifax Harbour, producing freezing spray that would sometimes result in an inch-and-a-half of ice on her mahogany hull. Daytime highs of five degrees Celsius in the cabin, despite a space-heater running 24/7 often left me with no other choice than to hide out at the local pub, and, less frequently, the library. I often faced a morning walk that began at 5:30 AM to make the one-hour trek across the MacDonald Bridge to where I still held my position as a meteorologist in

Halifax. The wind was brutal, and each day it wasn't long before I lost all ability to move my fingers. Survival was pivotal on the electric blanket I received that Christmas, which instantly catapulted my parents to super-star status. Thanks Mom, thanks Dad.

As a realist, I made no claim to the certainty of this voyage becoming a reality this particular autumn, but I was fully committed to doing everything within my power to supply and prepare my boat, safety-wise and otherwise, to make her completely seaworthy for possibly taking the Bermudian route to the eastern Caribbean, Cuba, or perhaps the Bahamas. With my intent, determination, enthusiasm, and assistance from fellow sailors, friends, and complete strangers, my journey had already begun.

§§§

Much had changed in a very short period of time. Just one year earlier, a few days after the purchase of *Annie Laurie,* I was on the verge of tears, wondering what I had gotten myself into. I had just received a phone call from a historic Halifax property that owned the wharf where Super Dave and I had tied her up a few days before. In no pleasant way, I was told to have the boat moved by suppertime. A forty-foot boat, and it hadn't occurred to me until that moment that I perhaps would need some assistance if I ever had to move her from A to B.

All the doubts started to flow, remembering everyone who had warned me that I might not be prepared to take on such a challenge. Perhaps they were right; I was not being practical, hoping to live on a boat with no place to keep her, and having no idea how to even dock her by myself.

Simon, a co-worker of mine, was completely understanding of my situation, having lived on a wooden ketch of his own in England some years ago. That day, after giving me a hand moving the boat to an alternate wharf, he assured me it would only be a matter of time, and I would get a better handle on things.

And that was true. The day eventually came when I had to leave the dock on my own. I cast off all but two lines, considered the wind and tide, and having the engine ready and the helm in place, I ran forward to cast off the bowline. I then proceeded aft to cast off the stern line. Turning around, I noticed the bow had become stuck between two pilings on the dock. But how important was that? The boat wasn't sinking, not even close. So what was the worry? I could learn by trial and error, and a bit of missing paint from the hull or a blob of tar donated from the wharf wouldn't cause irreparable damage. I was sure we were going to *go* places together. A few bumps and bruises to show her a world she, or myself, had never known, were easily looked after with a few painted bandages.

Now, one refit and a year later, I had decided to set sail for the tropics. I've learned that you just have to throw yourself into certain situations if you are ever to get the most out of life. It's daunting to say the least, and terrifying at times, but inspiration and encouragement is around every corner; whether through a new friendship, the challenge of a storm, another incredible display of nature, or by a unique moment you never in your life would have encountered if you had not taken the chances you had until now.

That inspiration, from whatever source, is what gets you through the seemingly hopeless times. Simon had a few other words that day I have not forgotten, and they are dedicated to those discouraging folks who say it cannot be done:

Get out of the way for those who are doing it!

Five

I made the decision to move to Lunenburg in late August. The town would have all the resources I would need for making preparations for my journey. I gradually fazed myself out of my forecasting position, and, having used my spare time over the previous winter to study for and acquire a 60-ton Captains license, I took on side work as captain for a local tour-boat company. As summer drew to a close, I eventually found myself working solely as a bartender in a local pub. It was then that I made a final decision on my destination, and signed on my first crew member, Tom. Young, enthusiastic, and years of sailing experience under his belt, I knew he'd be a perfect companion for a voyage to Cuba.

In addition to considering applications for additional crew, there were a million other things to contemplate, both big and small, to ensure this voyage would go smoothly: a handful of engine issues, a new coat of paint for the bottom, affix name boards, spare bulbs for navigational lights, insurance, life raft. And a most important question had to be answered: which route should I follow?

"Sure, sail to Bermuda on your way south. If she has been offshore, and you know every nut and every bolt and can envision her rolling over and coming back up relatively intact. If that's the case, then there are few reasons to take a safer, more time-consuming coastal route."

These were the words of advice from a highly respected captain. Captain Wayne was generous and genuine with sharing his experience of the north Atlantic in November. These waters are notoriously unpredictable in autumn, and I had been the subject of their wrath more than once during my days aboard tall ships. Instead of taking those near misses with death or serious injury into consideration, I was trying to suppress their memory, hoping to have a bit of luck on my side. This notion was encouraged by an acquaintance that had completed this run numerous times aboard his schooner. Here lies the key difference Captain Wayne was trying to highlight: This friend had owned his boat for many years and had sailed her extensively offshore. My boat? She'd never lost sight of Nova Scotia.

It could have been the case that everything could have gone smoothly. We could have had a beautiful run to Bermuda, where we'd be in a good position for making a shot south to the Virgin Islands, if I should decide to change my destination. Then again, we could have risked getting caught mid-way by terrible weather, with no place to run and hide.

I was never one to argue against the true pleasure of a journey being the journey itself, not the destination. Now that I had come to accept that the Bermuda route was less than ideal, I was then able to look forward to re-visiting some of the eastern U.S. ports I visited years earlier during my tall ship career.

While in Lunenburg that autumn, it wasn't all work and no play. Lunenburg hosted a Wednesday night classic boat race during the summer and fall, and for my first race, the wind was blowing twenty-five knots with gusts to thirty from the northwest. Boats taking part in the race danced around the invisible start-line waiting for the cannon signalling the start. It was just myself and Tom, out for his inaugural sail aboard *Annie Laurie*. With a lot of wind but not a lot of room to manoeuvre, my heart was in my mouth as we flew past the boats sitting idle on their moorings. We were just settling into a new course after tacking at the stern of the *Bluenose II* when a gust came and we heeled over further than I'd ever heeled before on my boat. Everything I had failed to properly lash to my cabin top went sliding towards the rail, and until Tom suggested I ease the sail out, the boat was sufficiently heeled to have the rudder out of the water, robbing me of steerage. Once the sail was eased, and the rudder was back in the water, I was able to veer off and avoid the sailboat a few meters ahead, with the screaming man waving his arms, believing I simply didn't see his 50-foot boat I was about to pulverize. These sorts of experiences were important in pointing out things I should change or improve before my big trip, and showed just how limited my experience was with small boats.

I had the opportunity to exercise my musical side around town that fall as well. Some new friends invited me to a jam session, and having neglected my Scottish smallpipes for quite some time, I jumped at the opportunity. Arriving on their doorstep early that evening, I realized immediately this visit was fate, as I was greeted by one who would become the third member of our crew.

Having arrived in Lunenburg two months ago, Nancy and Paul were doing her a favour by giving her a roof over her head, but it was time for her to move on. Never having sailed before, a few things were going through my mind. With no experience on a boat, you cannot know issues regarding seasickness, or their ability to deal with rough weather or other precarious situations. Everyone must start somewhere though, and I decided to go out on a bit of a limb and give her this chance to prove her capabilities.

Back on the boat that night, her curiosity about every last inch of the boat kept me up all night. She had to know every little detail. What's in there? What does this do? Is it always this cold? Can I have that blanket? Where's my bunk? She talked a lot, which was all right, as I myself am a woman of few words.

I knew what I was looking for in a crewmate, and I'd had many people approach me during those weeks, having heard rumours through the grapevine of available bunks to Cuba. I declined many offers, because I know that certain *feeling* that should be there, that instant rapport that cannot be explained, but can be easily recognized by its absence. Tom had it, and so did my new recruit.

Add to tomorrows list: food bowls, cat food, kitty litter.

§§§

I was procrastinating for about an hour after finishing my bartending shift. A southeasterly gale had the boats in the harbour bobbing around like corks, all of them holding on to their moorings for dear life, waiting for the worst to pass. I was exhausted from a poor nights sleep and lack of food. I knew it wasn't going to be easy rowing against that wind to get home after work, but I honestly didn't expect it to be impossible. Once I rowed out of the lee of the docks and was out in open water, I could not fight the wind and waves. I returned to the dock, bailed the water out of the dinghy, and commenced to sit on the dock, and wait for something to happen. My friend Rory from one of Lunenburg's tall ships, *Picton Castle*, came walking down the wharf. He wondered if I would like to come for dinner and a movie, and if need be, have a bunk for the night.

The rains were torrential and I was well prepared except for my lack of boots. Rory came back from the foc's'le with extra dry socks and shoes, and we set my drenched gear beside the antique cook stove, whose roaring fire was warming a batch of whiskey cider. The wind in the *Picton Castle*'s extensive rigging screamed louder as the night grew darker, and it left me a bit anxious as I envisioned my boat chaffing through her mooring lines and drifting, helpless, onto the rocks. But with a few sips of cider and a haddock and rice dinner on the way, my worries abated and I was in much better spirits.

Times like these, I would momentarily long for the simplicity of apartment living in Halifax, before quickly shaking myself of the thoughts and thanking my lucky stars I was no longer trapped by its quiet monotony.

§§§

The challenges would continue, and there would be days when I wholeheartedly believed that this trip was not meant to be, and that there was nothing I could do to overcome the brick walls that stood before me. Somehow though, when things seemed at their worst, the universe would cough up a rebuttal to my negativity, and things would begin to look up once more. Throughout my life, I've had to learn and relearn this perennial lesson; that with any situation in life, you can plan all you like and worry all you want, but things will never turn out as expected. Your life may take an unanticipated twist, but if you keep positive and let things flow, you will find the reason for what initially seems like a great difficulty. The things that defeat us now won't even come into play when the time comes for that dream to come true. They will be nothing but a distant memory, if in fact they can even be recalled at all.

It was always helpful to remember such ruminations when I hit those now-expected roadblocks. I would learn after that stormy night aboard *Picton Castle* that my only crew (aside from my new kitten Effie, named for the oldest Grand Banks fishing schooner still afloat) would be unable to make the journey to Cuba after all. We all have a road to follow and our own opportunities to pursue, and so I wished Tom all the best, then held my head in my hands, not knowing how I was ever going to find crew in these final hours.

Like clockwork, the evening after bidding Tom adieu, I received a phone call from a man introducing himself as Don. I would learn much later he'd been prompted by a concerned mutual friend who believed he'd be just the guy to talk me out of my impending self-inflicted catastrophe. On the contrary, Don called to offer all the help he could give. Having cruised Cuba aboard his steel schooner *Road to the Isles* for the last twelve winters, he was full of knowledge, excellent advice, common sense, and loads of encouragement. I would not solve the crew dilemma that evening, but I was filled with hope and confidence that my plans, no matter how little time remained, were preparing to fall into place.

I turned my attention to the routes and navigation that would lead me to Cuba. The more I viewed the charts, the closer I was to determining my route. It seemed to make good sense to make Gloucester, Massachusetts my first American port, where I would then motor through the Cape Cod Canal. Originally, I had intended a coastal sail the entire way, just detouring into port whenever the forecast suggested it would be prudent. It became appealing though, for a couple of reasons, to go down the Intracoastal Waterway, an often narrow sequence of rivers, canals, and sounds that takes you through relatively protected waters, beginning in Virginia and ending a thousand miles later in Miami. One reason was to avoid Cape Hatteras, which could be treacherous in autumn. The other reason was to visit my good friend and old shipmate from *Eye of the Wind*, Ben.

As I wrapped up my shifts at the bar, the weather was getting colder, the days shorter, and the pressure was on to get out of Lunenburg. I was planning to make my way to Surrette's Island at the southern tip of Nova Scotia, where I could take advantage of the massive tides to paint her bottom. The tidal range was sufficient enough that I could tie her to a wharf at high tide and she would be high and dry and ready for painting six hours later.

I felt on the verge of crumbling under the pressure, as my self-imposed departure date of October 20th came and went, and I fell short of reaching my goal. At times, I felt rendered completely immobile. Despite all the help I was being showered with from many different friends and strangers, providing me with information, books, charts, safety equipment, and the occasional tot, I still somehow felt utterly alone, and was not able to pin down why. All I knew was that I felt overwhelmed on the organizational side of things and with the decisions I had to struggle with, and ultimately make on my own.

So thank God for Ollie's Stress Free and Electrical Shed. Inspired by Ivan's Stress Free Bar in the Virgin Islands, a member of *Picton Castle*'s crew converted the ship's electrical shed on the wharf into a cozy and inspired gathering place for the crew to mingle and decompress. Its grand opening coincided very well with my latest breakdown, and I would spend many an evening in its warm embrace.

I was eventually able to cross some major items off my master list of preparations. Fuel filters, mast boots, jib boom, life rings and lights (though no life raft), varnish, paint, distilled water, kerosene... the list seemed endless but the end was now in sight. A local sail-maker repaired an old sail someone had donated, so I now had a small storm sail I could raise in an emergency, if all else failed, should I have found myself out in the weather I planned to avoid.

Meanwhile, Effie was settling in quite well. She had been seasick only once, and despite her clumsiness, she'd thus far managed to stay out of the water. My mother thought it was terrible I was subjecting a kitten to the rigors and risks of the sailing life, and so she picked up a small safety harness for her. At least one of us now stood a chance at survival should the unthinkable happen.

It was now October 26th, and I was now prepared to leave Lunenburg for Surrette's Island with the next two-day weather window. One last question remained: would I have crew?

I was aboard *Annie Laurie* on her mooring, having moved her off the dock due to an approaching southerly gale. It was still the calm before the storm at 9:00 PM when I heard a voice coming from out on the water. It was someone in a little rowboat, but because of the darkness, I couldn't for the life of me figure out who it was. We had a brief banter back and forth, and I nervously pretended to know exactly who owned that deep voice as he continued to row closer.

"It's Logan."

The crew I had been hoping for. I had met him at the September Classic boat race, and he and a friend had both expressed an interest in sailing to Cuba, though neither one possessed a phone, or had left me any contact information, or provided me with any certainty of their availability. I hadn't heard from him in weeks, and he was the only link to my other crew hopeful, Ed. I instantly felt relief, as I realized I wouldn't have to do any of the passage south on my own. I could once again be excited about it, instead of carrying the dread that had slowly been developing.

It seemed in many ways a long-time coming, but by the final crunch, things were finally beginning to take shape. The gale passed, and thirty-six hours later Logan and I were on our way down the coast to Surrette's Island, where Ed arrived two days later and together we painted the bottom of the boat. With that out of the way, and the next three days looking like an excellent weather window to cross the Bay of Fundy, we raised our sails, and set out into five foot seas on a beautiful beam reach. We said our final farewell to Nova Scotia, and watched the Cape Sable lighthouse gradually fade to black.

Part Two

A ship is safe in harbour, but that's not what ships are for.

William Shedd

Six

After close to eighty hours at sea, we made landfall in Provincetown, Massachusetts. That's about twenty-four hours longer than one would expect to make such a crossing, but it wasn't really a case of the boat living up to her nickname *Sea Plough*. It had more to do with the *unbelievable* tidal currents south of Nova Scotia.

We left Surrette's Island around noon in a strong northwesterly breeze and an ebbing tide. The tidal current was pushing us sideways at close to four knots. We just couldn't fight it, and as I realized our course was going to put us on Soldiers Ledge, I decided to alter course and just let the tide take us where it would. Dave, a friend at Surrette's Island, warned us of such tides, mentioning that we could be pulled as far south as Seal Island. Not that I didn't believe him (he'd lived and sailed in the area for thirty-five years) but I just couldn't imagine being pushed over ten miles in the wrong direction. But pushed we were, and we ended up passing within a quarter mile of Blonde Rock, the southernmost hazard to navigation in Nova Scotia, and *twenty miles* off our intended course.

The forecast had called for light to moderate northwesterly winds, which meant we didn't expect any more than twenty knots. Most of the trip the winds were a solid twenty to twenty-five, at times gusting to over thirty knots, and the building seas, at times combined with tidal rips, made for uncomfortable conditions. Effie rid herself of her breakfast early on, and her queasy facial expressions and glazed-over eyes told me she was seriously questioning why she hadn't jumped ship in Surrette's Island while she still had the chance.

The crossing was hard on all of us; too rough to sleep, all of our clothes soaked, and it was next to impossible to keep the stove going and balance the kettle and pots and pans while trying to keep from being thrown around ourselves. Until now, I was used to sailing on larger boats when in such weather, where the motion was far less violent. It was Ed's first experience offshore in any kind of boat, and he handled it like a true Maritimer, his spirits always high. We learned to get by on one or two hour rests, not sleep, by just laying down with eyes closed, in a state of delirium. Arriving in Provincetown at sunset, we were cold and tired, and moving along under engine power alone since the wind had died in the final hours. I just wanted to find a place to anchor and go to sleep, but Ed wanted our arrival to be poignant and memorable, so we set all the sails, and did a one-boat Parade of Sail along Provincetown's waterfront, as Ed nodded and smiled back at me from the bow, "*That's* how you come into P-town!"

The approach of Hurricane Noel forced us to stay in Provincetown for a few days. Noel was downgraded to a tropical storm by the time it reached Cape Cod, but as Ed and I watched a boat sink at it's mooring, and the winds having not yet reached their maximum predicted strength of seventy knots, we felt cause for concern. That's when the Provincetown Harbourmaster, seeing us at anchor and pinching our pennies, kindly offered us free docking in a space belonging to the schooner *Hindu,* who was already well on her way to Key West for the winter.

The calm after the storm quickly ensued, and we set out for the Cape Cod Canal twenty miles away. Timing is critical when arriving at the East Entrance of the canal. The advice I'd been given made it clear that by arriving at the entrance as the tide was rising, we would have the proper current to transit the five mile pass in about half an hour. The current, at its peak, could run eight knots, so with *Annie Laurie's* maximum speed of six knots under power, if the current was flowing in the opposing direction, we would still be losing ground.

I knew something was wrong as we entered the turbulence at the beginning of the narrows. We had been motoring a steady five and a half knots, but as I watched the speed on the GPS drop from five knots, to four, and eventually to less than one knot, we knew we had hit the tides wrong, and were in for a losing battle. We made a 180 degree turn, and our speed instantly increased to six knots with the engine in slow ahead. Having noticed a marina just off the canal a few minutes earlier, we thought it would be a good place to layover. It was slightly unnerving as we tried to get through the little gap in the sea wall, the current pushing so hard that I was forced to throttle her up to 2000 rpm and aim not for the gap, but for the concrete wall beside it. Once inside, all was calm, and there was little indication in this hideaway of the raging currents just meters to the north.

Here, we regrouped and waited for the tide, which meant we had four hours to wander around the town of Sandwich and pick up some fruits and vegetables and the ever-important supply of dark chocolate. While Ed cooked dinner, we got underway again, motoring through the cold and dark, until we were eventually spit out the west exit of the Canal. Our original destination when setting out from P-Town that morning was to make New Bedford, but it was close to midnight and New Bedford was still many miles away, so we decided to seek out a safe anchorage somewhere closer. The town of Marion seemed to have a well-marked channel, so we altered course.

The buoys marking the channel were unlit, so with the spotlight, we scanned the harbour entrance for the charted buoys, but somehow missed them. When the spotlight fell onto a rocky shoreline about fifty feet ahead, I throttled back to slow-ahead, and we carefully traced the shoreline until we found one of the channel marks. We had missed the first three, and were a precarious half-mile outside the channel.

Marion is an avid sailing community, and despite being late in the sailing season, there were upwards of a hundred boats still moored in the harbour. Many empty moorings as well provided the added challenge of dodging their attached floating lines, which could have fouled in the propeller. We were relieved to tie up to the first wharf we could find.

§§§

The next morning, we finally cleared customs after a week in the States, for which I received a scolding and stern warning. There were no Customs officers in Provincetown, but apparently we were meant to at least place a phone call to the nearest Customs office, to make arrangements to clear when we arrived in an official Port of Entry. Technically, said Officer

McAllister, he should seize my boat. I bit my tongue; *just play the game.* As I stood down below with the officer, looking over his shoulder at the boys sitting on deck in the cockpit, all it would have taken was one wrong look from Ed, and I would have burst into laughter. Officer McAllister, bald by choice and no stranger to the gym, was professional and only doing his job, so I played along.

"Yes, sir, I'm terribly sorry, sir. I'll know for next time, sir." Without too much more ado and a payment of $19, I received my cruising permit, and *Annie Laurie* was now legal in American waters for one year.

Logan headed home, as planned, and Ed and I departed Marion the morning of November 10th, vaguely aiming for Newport, Rhode Island. Once out in Buzzards Bay, we decided the wind was not in our favour, and that it would be more interesting to head to Martha's Vineyard. We passed through a tricky area known as Woods Hole at the proper tide, and we sailed into Vineyard Haven just before sunset. Upon going ashore, we were appalled and shocked to discover that America has places known as 'dry towns'. We were told it was a few miles to Oak Bluffs, where we would find both the nearest bars and liquor stores. We decided not to waste another moment, and we began the hike. Three miles later, our efforts were rewarded with locally brewed pumpkin ale and homemade New

England clam chowder.

We sailed the following morning for Block Island, Rhode Island. We were determined during those days to motor as little as possible, so despite the passage from the Vineyard to Block Island being only thirty miles, it took us twenty-four hours. We were tired and very cold at sunrise as we wrapped around the north of the island to approach the harbour on the west side, but we felt very privileged by the night time sights, which day sailors would know nothing of. The dolphins had come out to play, and the phosphorescent impressions of their bodies as they danced around the boat were surreal. We also had the opportunity to practice our skills in recognizing the light patterns of the shipping traffic, necessary in total darkness to discern the difference between a tanker, tug, barge, or pilot boat.

We almost managed to sail the entirety of the narrow channel into the western harbour, but the wind came around and we had to fire up the engine for a few minutes, to avoid landing on the beach about fifteen feet to our right. We eyed up a dock in the inner harbour, and decided to go alongside rather than anchor. Ed was up in the rig, a better vantage point for keeping an eye on water depths. The water was very clear, the bottom sandy and white, and at times it looked like there shouldn't be enough water beneath us to float the boat. So when we felt the little nudge, and she came to a halt about fifty feet from the dock, we weren't too surprised. Ed suggested setting a sail to heel us over, the wind being favourable to blow us off the underwater beach and back into deeper water. But before we could do anything, the wind on just the hull itself was sufficient to do the job. We slipped off the shoal, and cast our lines onto the wharf.

Ed talked about writing a cruising guide to sailing out-of-season. Everywhere we visited seemed to be packed-up and dismantled for the winter. Block Island was no exception; it was conspicuously desolate. The island was covered with expensive summer homes, owned mostly by folks who seem to prefer sunsets over sunrises, as the west side of the island holds the majority of the New England-style cedar-shingled cottages. There is only one town, on the east side, where all the tourist shops were closed, the post office was open from 10:00 AM until 1:00 PM a couple days a week, and the grocery store was locked up by 6:00 PM. There was one main road that circled the island, and it took a mere two hours to do a full circumnavigation by bicycle, including the stops made at a few centuries-old lighthouses.

We waited out a nasty nor'easter before biting the bullet and motoring out into high seas, with the forecast promising things to diminish throughout the day. We had struggled a bit with the decision of whether to go inside of Long Island Sound, or just go directly to Cape May, New Jersey. A friend's advice was to go outside the sound, avoid the shipping traffic and hassles of the Coast Guard when passing the security zones around New York City. I was inclined to take his advice, adding to my own argument that I didn't have detailed charts for the Sound.

We passed Montauk Point at the eastern tip of Long Island around noontime. We had great wind for the next six hours, and we calculated, at this rate, we would be in Cape May the following evening. The wind heard my estimate, then quietly and promptly packed its things and left. We sat in the cockpit, becalmed, before receiving the next forecast indicating strong southwesterly winds approaching. As night fell, the seas began to build, heavy rains began to fall, and we found ourselves with significantly reduced visibility from rain and fog in the New York traffic lanes[4]. Not equipped with radar, our only hope was that our small radar reflector would make us visible on the radars of the constant stream of container ships, which populate the approaches to New York City.

The boat was feeling over-pressed with the amount of sail we had set, so I grabbed my harness and went forward to take the mainsail down. While doing this, a little green light appeared ahead of us. It can be

---

[4] There are traffic separation schemes on the ocean, generally at the entrance to any busy harbour, to keep inbound and outbound commercial traffic safely divided.

very confusing in fog, darkness and high seas, trying to identify what exactly you might be looking at. The lights of another ship contain the information to tell you which way they're going, and some indication of the size of the vessel, but it's often difficult to tell how far away it is, and how fast it's going. After studying the bobbing green light for about ten seconds, I determined it was a sailboat, and was very close by. I went back and grabbed our bright spotlight, and shone it on them, then shone it on our rig, so they would have a better idea of what they were encountering too. They shone their spotlight back, in acknowledgement, and I determined they had the right-of-way, so we altered course. It's strange to be a hundred miles offshore, with so much ocean around, then to pass within a hundred feet of another small sailboat. Ed and I agreed it was uplifting to see another sailboat, experiencing exactly what we were experiencing, and probably just as cold, wet, tired, and seasick as we were.

Later the following evening, the winds and waves had subsided, and we once again found ourselves becalmed. What should have been a forty-eight hour passage became four days and three nights. It was nice, though, to finally be out of sight of land for a while. The days felt completely different. My mind wasn't cluttered with the worries of navigating around shoals and rocks and shoreline. The water was a minimum of two hundred feet deep, so I really did breathe a sigh of relief when out on open water. Instead of running up and down the companionway, plotting positions, we were instead sitting in the cockpit, reading books, writing letters, and working on 'baggy wrinkles' for chafe gear to prevent any more wear on the sails where they lay on the shrouds (the wire stays supporting the masts). When the weather was fine, a lot of this time was spent in a comfortable silence, though we'd occasionally delve into conversations of what was to come, and what we missed about home. Ed would talk about his girlfriend, and what she was up to and their future plans in Nova Scotia. I mostly just thought about the boat, our route, and what was going to happen next. I frequently imagined different scenarios, and how we would deal with various emergency (or non-emergency) situations.

One such situation occurred as we passed Atlantic City, New Jersey on our last morning of our four-day transit from Block Island to Cape May. I had gone to bed at 5:00 AM after taking the bulk of the night watch. It was rough once again, and I was cozy down below in my sleeping bag, warm and dry. I could hear the sound of water sloshing along the hull, it sounded like we were making good speed. The sloshing seemed clearer somehow than what I was accustomed to, and I briefly envisioned the water on the wrong side of the hull. I can be an excessive worrier at times, so this time I forced my overactive imagination into submission, and went back to enjoying the cosiness of my down sleeping bag. With the next gust of wind, the boat heeled over, and my eyes were drawn to the corner by the icebox where water was bubbling up from beneath the floorboards.

It could have been one of a couple things. I did have a bilge pump on board, which pumps automatically when the water reaches a certain level, and it could have been the case that it was pumping like mad and there was still a large amount of water coming aboard from a large leak somewhere. I may have panicked if that thought had crossed my mind, but I didn't think about that scenario until later. Alternatively, it could have been that the water was coming in at its regular rate (yes, for a wooden boat, that is normal), but the bilge pump wasn't pumping for some reason. I assumed the bilge pump had burned out, because it had been making unusual noises the day before, which, for whatever reason, I had chosen to ignore. This turned out to be the case. It took us a little while to pump out using the manual pump in the cockpit, because it was clogged as well. Once we got it cleaned out, we were able to pump the bilge dry, and later take the automatic pump apart and remove the rubber band that had caused its breakdown.

One small crisis out of the way, I decided I would dig out the detailed chart for the approaches to Cape May. It didn't take long to discover we didn't actually have it aboard. We were about five miles off the New Jersey coast with eighteen miles left to go. I was considering winging it, assuming that any hazards to navigation would probably be clearly marked by buoys, or would be indicated on the large-scale chart. I thought about other resources we had at our disposal. We had a VHF radio, and maybe there was someone we could call for advice; I wasn't too proud. Besides, I reasoned, it could possibly avoid a later search and rescue operation. I called the Cape May Coast Guard station on Channel 16, to request any information they could provide. I explained that we were a Canadian vessel just west of buoy R2, approaching Cape May without proper charts, and asked if there were any hazards we should be aware of. I gave him our co-ordinates and true course, and he said he'd plot it and get back to us. A few minutes later he called back, in a professional and deep tone, to say there were no shoals or wrecks, and our course would give us a safe approach to the breakwater. He added to this statement, "That said, ma'am, you are solely responsible for the safe navigation of your vessel". I acknowledged and thanked him, which he followed up in a more casual tone, "But, you know, if you have any other questions or concerns, please don't hesitate to contact us again." Ed imagined his name to be Gil, and I agreed. He sounded quite debonair.

The breakwater at the entrance provided a

daunting approach, with two knots of tidal current opposing us. Steering was tricky, and the channel was narrow. The night seemed darker than usual somehow, and the light from the spotlight seemed to fall dead before lighting the hazards we were hoping to avoid. We had a cruising guide that detailed the inner harbour, though not to scale. We used the spotlight to find our marks, many of them unlit, and we just hoped not to run aground, as the cruising guide talked about the necessity of frequent dredging to keep the waterways navigable. We managed to find a dock and tied up safe and sound by 8:00 PM. We hardly had the opportunity to shut the engine down when we were greeted by another Canadian heading south with his boat. Jean-Paul invited us over for wine, and we learned about his goodwill mission to Haiti. The top deck of his motorboat was loaded with bicycles to donate, and if I had paid more attention in French class during elementary school, I might know more about his journey.

We quietly left the dock bright and early the next morning and motored a mile or two to an anchorage. We sounded the bottom in a few areas with the lead-line (more precisely, a rock on a string), finding the depth the good old-fashioned way. It was a crowded area, so we felt we'd lucked out when a couple who had just hauled their boat for the winter kindly offered us their mooring. We stayed for a few more days to make sure the bilge was clean, the pump was working, and to wait for another crewmember, Ed's sister, Justine. We met a lovely Canadian couple, Mike and Jan, along with their beagle Beauty, aboard their small sloop *Pathos*. We shared a couple of great evenings, drinking wine and cooking dinner for each other, and sharing stories of our journeys and struggles thus far. Before leaving Cape May, we arrived back at the boat after an afternoon ashore, and the entire starboard side was loaded with groceries. Rice, beans, pasta, apples, oranges, peas, you name it. We never had the opportunity to thank them or say goodbye, but we were sure we'd see them again someday, somewhere down the blue highway.

Seven

Justine arrived late in the evening but ahead of schedule, not knowing where to find the boat. Of the many docks and marinas, she coincidentally asked the cab driver to drop her off at the one across the street from where we were moored. I happened to be on a payphone there, and after only a few weeks in the States, it was pretty easy to spot a Canadian. We had never met, neither of us knew what the other looked like, and she walked right up and interrupted my phone call with, "Are you Laura? Oh thank God!"

Winds weren't favourable and charts were scarce for heading up the Delaware Bay, so we decided to head offshore and go directly to Norfolk, Virginia. It was miserable weather when we left New Jersey, rainy and windy and cold. Once outside the breakwater, we could add rough seas to the list. It was great wind for making progress, but it was not so easy on our stomachs. I commended Justine for not 'swallowing the anchor' after that first passage with us. It was as bad as any hazing ritual one could imagine, but the beckon of Cuba allowed us to overcome the temporary discomforts, no matter how great.

Ed decided to head home to Nova Scotia after arriving in Norfolk. I understood his reasons and was appreciative of the fact that he was so open with me about his intentions and that he made sure he wasn't leaving me in a bind. We didn't know each other very well when he joined the boat in Surrette's Island, and I was relying on the recommendation of a couple of friends that he would be excellent crew. He had so much initiative when it came to taking care of the boat and getting things done, and was very attentive, responsible, and reliable with navigation. He was absolutely everything my friends said he would be and more, and I would miss him.

It was his wish to be rowed across to the other wharf for a final voyage in the dinghy, even though we were actually dockside at the time. Justine and I said our goodbyes and got back in the dinghy. Due to my knot-job when we got back to the mothership that night, when we awoke in the morning, the dinghy was gone. As much as I complained about how ugly it was, and how it was next to impossible to row in a straight line, it was nevertheless a necessary thing to have. Justine and I borrowed a dinghy and did an extensive search down the eastern branch of the Elizabeth River where the north winds of the last few days would have likely carried it, but we returned empty handed. It would become an epic quest in the coming weeks, the search for a new, suitable rowing dinghy. It had to happen soon, as we would be anchoring more and more as dock fees went up as we continued south, and we'd need a dinghy if we ever wanted to go ashore.

Norfolk marked Mile Zero on the Intracoastal Waterway (ICW). It would be a welcomed break from the Atlantic, for however long we chose to follow it, with many interesting stops, the chance to anchor and sleep every night, and more riveting scenery. Our first stop was my friend Ben's place, just north of the Great Bridge Lock. Ben and his wife Brigid were so welcoming and provided us with every comfort. A cozy home to have showers, do laundry, wonderful dinners, bottomless glasses of wine, a car to run errands, and a cozy bed for a couple nights reprieve from a damp chilly boat. I caught a glimpse of the family life as we all played in the backyard with L'il Bud, their Chesapeake Bay retriever, and thought about how it'd be many years, if ever, that I would find myself in a similar domestic situation. The two short days we spent there ended too soon, and Ben was there to cast off our lines after we made a call to the tender of the Great Bridge lock to inform them of our intent to catch the next lock opening.

There was naturally more boat traffic in the

ICW than out in the open ocean, and many passing boats offered an ego boost for the boat, with their thumbs up and hollers of *'Such* a pretty boat!' Justine and I were proud and really enjoyed the attention. We had more incentive everyday to make as many improvements as we could. Painting and tying on the baggy wrinkles were at the top of the list, as they were easy jobs to complete while the boat was underway. The gradual improvement in the weather as we reached warmer climes helped to make all these tasks more pleasure than chore.

Navigating down the narrow waterway proved to be challenging and a bit more stressful than I had anticipated. We were somewhat dependent on random advice from passing boats, such as the gentleman at the dock one day who said "Look out for the second red mark at the mouth of the Alligator River after mile marker 80, stay to the green... even if you're in the middle of the channel, you will go aground. The dredge hasn't made it out to re-dredge the channel." If it wasn't for such incidences, then we surely would have been aground more times than we already had. Our record was five groundings in one day, I believe. Some groundings were worse than others in terms of how stuck we were, and for how long, but we always eventually managed to use the engine to power ourselves off the mud banks. It was all mud in that area of the waterway, so running aground was not a serious matter; it just had the potential to create a great inconvenience if we were to become stuck for long periods of time. Our worst grounding occurred when we were under full sail and well within the boundaries of the channel. It's impossible to know the depths for certain without an electronic depth-sounder (though we had upgraded to at least a proper lead line and could now retire the rock on a string) and had we had one, we could have watched the gradual decrease in depth, and realized we should have adjusted our course more towards the middle of the channel.

We approached Oriental a couple of hours before sunset, and motored around the anchorage and docks looking for a good spot. Without a dinghy, we were ideally looking for a dock so we didn't have to swim ashore, and Oriental did have a free town dock. On our way to the dock, we came to a halt. *Aground.* We were stuck there long enough to watch two other boats motor by, and tie up to the only remaining spots on the town dock. A friendly Brit named Mark tried very hard to accommodate us by moving his boat *Jem* as much as he could to make room on the small wharf, but when I tried pulling in ahead of him, there was not enough water, and again, we were aground. Once we pushed ourselves out of there, we tried the other side of the wharf, where the locals said it *might* be deep enough. It wasn't. What I wouldn't do for a free parking space.

We gave up and went out to the anchorage. It was crowded with other cruisers, and I found a narrow spot between an American boat and a Danish boat. I snugged a bit closer to the Danish boat, and we were aground one last time for the day. Justine threw the anchor over for looks, and we went below for dinner and went to sleep.

In the morning Mark called us on the VHF to let us know he was leaving the town dock, so we could sneak in for forty-eight hours of dockage. Oriental served us well, and a few days later we had our new dinghy. Feeling prepared to head offshore once again, we motored four more hours down the ICW (with no more groundings) before reaching Beaufort, where we left the protection of the waterway and headed back out into the open Atlantic.

§§§

We felt we were off to a great start as we left the ICW from the inlet at Beaufort, North Carolina. Once offshore, a strong westerly breeze kept our speed up to 6 knots for hours. It seemed we would be around Cape Fear in no time, and into Charleston late the next evening.

Then we learned a little something about the Gulf Stream.

The wind continued to increase, and early on

our second day at sea, we had strong north-westerlies. We had both noticed the change in the water, primarily its warmth, but also the abundance of a certain kind of seaweed that is indicative of the Stream. It's around this time that things start to go a bit hazy; I don't fully recall my decision-making processes, or what I thought our situation was, or how I was reading the various signs. I think I doubted for a long time that we were in fact in the Gulf Stream, as I never thought it would be so close to shore. I'd heard many warnings about finding yourself in the Gulf Stream in a northerly wind, and the winds were already veering to the north, and the seas were building, and breaking frequently.

Somewhere, sometime, one by one I guess, sails started ripping. The line holding the clew (one of the corners) of the jib to the boom snapped, and that was it for the jib. I went up on the foredeck to try and tie it back on with another line, but it was flogging around madly, and when the bow struck a wave, and I went underwater to my waist as I clung desperately to the mast, I thought, *this is ridiculous.* The downhaul for the jib was in the cockpit, so Justine pulled the sail down, and we left it at that. I decided to let the sail go, allowing it to flog around at will, and bit by bit over the following days, we watched it go to pieces. I wasn't risking going forward again unless it was absolutely necessary. In moments like these, you don't really think about the monetary value of such items, despite their necessity for the trip south to continue. Well, you don't think about it when one sail goes, but then when the mizzen sail busts to shreds and the reef point in the mainsail tears a two-foot hole in it, such things do begin to cross your mind. But safety of the crew and getting into the nearest safe port are first and foremost.

What was frustrating for the first twenty-four hours was trying to make our way west. We were eighty miles offshore, and southeast of Cape Fear's Frying Pan Shoals and all we wanted to do was head back toward the continent. No matter how hard we tried, including motor-sailing and steering a course of due west, we were going due *south*, in a current that runs four knots in a *northerly* direction! South is good, but eighty miles out when all you want to see is land, west (or at *least* southwest) is much better. I just couldn't understand. I feel dense for not having gotten my head around it sooner. Perhaps lack of sleep, perhaps fear of the situation we were in, the incredible burden of responsibility I suddenly felt knowing I had another life in my hands... maybe all these things prevented me from accurately assessing the situation.

Night was falling on Day Two, waves were frequently sweeping the entire boat and filling the cockpit with water, Effie was meowing so loudly and mournfully, terrified and locked down below, and the wind was gale force. It still bothers me to think of the sound of the wind in the rigging during those days.

Justine later told me, that night as the sun disappeared below the horizon, all she could think was, 'There it goes… and it has to go *all* the way around the world again before it comes up. That's so far to go!' It was truly an awful feeling.

It was the longest night of my life, for certain, and I think Justine's too. There was no moon, and the clouds began to hide the stars early in the evening. I could hardly bring myself to look at the waves, what little I could make of them from the whitecaps after they broke. But the seas were becoming confused, coming from the west as well as the north, and it seemed important to watch each and every one, and to steer into them rather than letting them hit the boat from the side. Of course, neither of us slept. We took turns going down below for two hours each, and the rest of the time we were on deck together, just for moral support. Although I was clipped in while Justine rested below, she said that every time she heard a wave break over the boat, she would lay there, waiting for some sign that the boat was back on a good course, and that there was still a hand at the helm.

About an hour before sunrise, the boat lit up with an orange glow. We looked off the stern, and there was a flare in the sky. Someone had fired a flare, perhaps from a vessel in distress, what else would it be? This remains one of the most disturbing parts of the passage. I tried calling the coast guard, but we were too far out for them to pick up our radio signal. We were concerned for our own safety at this point, still struggling to break out of the Stream, shaking from cold, and seasickness and lack of rest and our inability to eat anything for the last 48 hours, so how could we possibly turn around to investigate? We couldn't, yet it greatly distressed us, the thoughts that another small boat not unlike our own was in trouble, and people had fired the flare as a last attempt to call for help. We saw a container ship a few hours later, and tried to relay a message to them, but with no response. It haunts me.

In the morning, the waves had grown only slightly from what they were at final light the night before. The wind was now a northeasterly gale, and I finally realized that we were in some sort of counter-current, running off the edges of the Stream itself, in the opposite direction. Now, with that mystery finally figured out, came the decision to run with it; to turn the boat southwest rather than northwest, and start surfing. This is where I approached the limits of my experience on small boats. It seemed a bit precarious to me, putting such massive waves behind the boat. It seemed like they could 'catch-up' with us, and as they were still breaking often, I felt they had the potential to roll the boat over as we surfed down their sides. Perhaps there was no danger of that at all, and that's my inexperience talking; I worry about things I don't know about, and often come up with the worst possible scenario.

I called down to Justine that I was turning the boat around and the motion was going to feel a lot different in a minute. I waited for a lull in the waves, the most that could be expected in such conditions, and spun the boat around. For the next eighteen hours, it took so much energy and concentration to keep her stern to the waves, and not allow us to become broadside to the swells. It was a constant state of vigilance, alternately looking at the compass and then looking behind. We often got warning waves, ones that would crash close behind us, then would be followed by a train of the three largest waves of the last ten minutes. The sea was kind in this manner, because we were delirious and our minds would wander and eyes would close until we would hear these periodic wake-up calls.

Once the wind was behind us, I decided to set a sail. We still had one left to work with, after all. I set the genoa before realizing the bottom shackle holding the tack of the sail had fallen off. Justine hauled it back in, and we set the mainsail, double-reefed, since the single reef was torn, and this helped us remain more balanced and allowed us to throttle back the engine a bit and conserve our waning fuel.

Through it all we managed to keep our sense of humour and positive attitude. A visit from the Gulf Stream dolphins helped to lift spirits. Gulf Stream dolphins are unlike the ones in Nova Scotia. For one thing, they're huge. They're rambunctious and energetic, and it wears you out to watch them. I saw a few Portuguese man-of-wars, the highly poisonous jellyfish with 'sails' on their backs that extend out of the water. At one point Justine yelled down to ask me if it was possible that there were hummingbirds way out here. She had seen her first flying fish.

Those four days will forever be known in our personal histories as the Terrible Horrible No Good Very Bad Days, thanks to Justine's likening them to Judith Viorst's children's story. Through those four days, I never felt like we weren't going to make it; it was just knowing what we had to face between *now* and *land* that was difficult. The boat took an awful beating, far worse than anything I'd ever put her through, and likely worse than what her previous two owners had as well. There was always that uncertainty, that she had not been put to the test like this before, and despite my every effort in the last year to make her sound and seaworthy, perhaps I had missed something.

But here we were in Charleston, having arrived at sunrise on Day 4. Safe and sound, and three days later, we were getting back to our old selves. We would get up early and go for a walk, then come back to the boat and buckle down to work. We replaced worn-out halyards and other lines, stitched sails, made chafe gear, put mousings on shackles; we did absolutely everything that came to mind, so there was nothing left for Neptune to say 'Ah-ha, but you forgot about *this*!'

Most of my thoughts during those days at sea, as I chanted aloud for the sea to let go of the boat and let us out of the Stream, were of Nova Scotia. It was a tremendous comfort to remember the last place my feet had been on her shores, and I swore if I ever made it safely back home, I would never set out this far from Scotian soil again.

Eight

Time heals almost everything, and with the passing of a few days, the shock of our experience began to fade, and with one random encounter, things began to look up. While walking down the Charleston docks on our way back to the dinghy to row out to the mothership, I decided to swing by a boat that had the deck lights I'd been looking for, hoping to find out where he got them. We approached the fellow aboard with the line, 'Hey, nice spreader lights'. He tried to tell us his name was Mark, but we're sure it was his alias for Santa.

Within ten minutes of meeting Mark, it was decided that our sails would be taken to the nearest North Sails loft for repair, and he outfitted our boat with many things we should have had aboard, but didn't have the means, such as two new harnesses with inflatable life jackets, and binoculars we could actually discern shapes and colors through. He bought us wood and a hand plane for various unfinished projects, including a name board for the dinghy, which we had decided to name *James* (*Home*, James! *And don't spare the horses*!). Then, as if that weren't enough, we were offered a berth at the finest marina we'd encountered on the entire trip. He welcomed us on his boat, to use email and make the long-distance phone calls home, watch movies, and of course great meals and company. Even Effie took to wandering over, and before long started spending the nights there.

And he wasn't the only one. Jeff and Jodi lived aboard their sailboat in the marina, and I was dumbfounded at their generosity as they loaned us their EPIRB, insisting we keep it until *Annie Laurie* was safely home in Nova Scotia. EPIRB stands for Emergency Position Indicating Radio Beacon, and if I were to find myself in a perilous situation, a flick of a switch would send a signal via satellite to the Coast Guard, and search and rescue would know exactly where to find us. Jodi arrived with the beacon, having already made the arrangements of changing the information that would be made available to the Coast Guard, should we pull that switch. This included the name of the vessel, port of registry, and its general specifications. This provided us with incredible peace of mind, as our communication system aboard was limited to a VHF radio, which is only effective for reaching other ships that are in your line of sight. The digital signal from the EPIRB on the other hand, could be detected from anywhere on earth.

Our Cape Fear experience gave us that extra push we needed to go over some essential safety training. Justine tried on an immersion suit, used in abandon ship scenarios, to get a feel for their awkwardness and to learn the important details involved in donning one. For example, if you don't make the effort to expel the extra air in the waterproof suit before you zip it up, air can end up in your feet, making it next to impossible to keep your head above water once you're immersed. Since we had the convenience of being dockside, we took the opportunity to remove almost everything from the boat, to dry-out on the dock in the sun, and to reorganize everything that had dislodged itself from its proper storage place during the violent motions offshore. We did a bit more painting and oiling of bare wood, and spliced new lifelines, which we could now clip onto with our new harnesses. We had a few spectators through the week as we did our maintenance, including a Ukrainian sailor who seemed impressed by our lack of male company on our endeavour.

"No mans? Why no mans?" he asked. I don't know how we did it, but somehow the boat continued to see great improvement, and traveled hundreds of miles, without mans.

After nine days in Charleston, the boat and crew

good as new, we set sail to wherever the wind would take us, which turned out to be St. Augustine, Florida, the oldest city in America. After four days in St. Augustine, we still hadn't met anyone *from* there, but it was certainly gorgeous to walk the historic streets, all of which have the distinctly Spanish feel about them. The famous Fountain of Youth beckoned to us, but after arriving at the end of Ponce De Leon Boulevard to find they charged $7 each to enter the park, it somehow seemed beyond our budgets at the time. We took a photo of a fountain at the entrance instead, which was probably similar. On the walk home, we passed numerous pawnshops, each with a variety of guns in the windows, reminding us just how far we were from Nova Scotia.

The dinghy Police took their jobs very seriously in St Augustine, especially if you tied your dinghy in a restricted area by accident, such as a marina. We were perplexed after returning to the marina early one morning after a night at the A1A Brewery, and *James* was in shackles. Apparently we were meant to register and pay $10 to leave our dinghy there. I felt indignant at what these people had done to *James* without giving us a simple warning as first time offenders. On principle, I had to find another way out of this situation. I walked the docks until I spotted a boat with a gentleman still awake at this late hour, watching a movie. I knocked, and he lent me some wire cutters. It turned out they were too small for the job (or that I was *only a weak woman!)* so we looked for other options, eventually realizing that the seat of our new dinghy (around which the chain was wrapped) was actually easily removed with a screwdriver. I went and traded the wire cutters for a screwdriver, and removed the seat. I ran back to return the tool as the dinghy Police were walking down the far dock. Once he realized what we had done, he began running like a mall cop in our direction. Justine pushed the dinghy off the dock as I jumped in, the dinghy cop angrily cursing and asking how we would like it if he phoned the police. Justine called back, "Our Captain... He didn't tell us anything about a fee! He'll be in to speak with you first thing in the morning." We hoped it wasn't the only dinghy dock in town.

We planned to spend Christmas there, and wait for the arrival of Don and his family aboard *Road to the Isles*, as we heard they were due to arrive in a few days. A change of plans took Justine back to Nova Scotia on Boxing Day, and I was left to complete the passage to Cuba alone.

Returning to the boat after seeing Justine to a cab, I spent my first night alone since leaving Lunenburg. I found it hard to be in St Augustine for Christmas. I was supposed to be in Cuba by now, after all. I tried to at least appreciate the fact that I was in warmer climates. One year earlier there was an inch of ice on the hull as she sat dockside in Dartmouth. *That* was a miserable existence. I really did have something to be thankful for.

I reminisced about that first night underway, sitting on deck alone as Ed and Logan slept below, as I watched the last corner of Nova Scotia disappear into the darkness. I remember that feeling of *I'm really doing it! My journey has begun!* Now, as I sat feeling trapped in the St Augustine anchorage, believing I'd be unable to get further south on my own, I no longer spent hours of my day planning the next jump. My thoughts now ruminated on my reasons for doing this trip in the first place, and why I made certain choices without really thinking them through, ones I felt I was bound to regret.

I had to nip this self-pity in the bud. It was time to put out a call for crew. I posted my ad for any experienced sailors interested in sailing at least to Key West, and perhaps to Cuba. Mans or womans. And if mans, to please apply with photo.

§§§

I finally met Don and family in person a few days after Justine's departure, and with a bit of encouragement and reassurance, I was prepared to attempt a couple hundred miles on my own. I made my way from St Augustine to West Palm Beach, where my sister Katie joined me. Yes, the same Katie who, when asked in September to help me sail from Nova Scotia to Cuba, responded, "That old wooden thing? She'll never make it..." The weather was certainly nice and the waters warm upon her arrival in Florida.

We hopped our way down the coast to Key Biscayne, where the water was finally crystal clear, and giant starfish were readily visible twenty-five feet below the surface. I had long anticipated my first dive into warm, clear tropical water from my own boat. I had wondered what would be significant about it that would make it memorable, so it would stand out in the years to come against subsequent swims.

Upon anchoring mid-afternoon in Key Biscayne, Katie was attempting to make everything all ship-shape before we could relax and enjoy what remained of the afternoon and evening. She dropped the deck-wash bucket over the side to retrieve some water, but as she hauled it back up, the knot let go and the line slipped off, and the bucket started to float away. It was a big white bucket whose original use was to store Tancook sauerkraut. After a brief argument over who dropped the bucket versus who had tied the poor knot, I jumped in, and thus my first swim in Florida waters would be forever etched in my brain. What could be more memorable than looking up at your little wooden boat, with a backdrop of palm trees and a slowly cooling sunset, and to be cradling an empty five-gallon bucket once abundant with good old Nova Scotian sauerkraut?

We were finally feeling tropical, and a mere two hundred miles of easy sailing was all that remained between Cuba and us. As we made our way down the Florida Keys to Key West, singing along to the Beach Boys on the radio and trying to figure out the exact location of Kokomo, our excitement over Cuba grew.

We stopped in Marathon, which was little more than an expensive floating trailer park community. It was, and remains, beyond me why many cruisers, year after year, make Marathon their winter destination. The water was too dirty for swimming, there was no beach, and once out of the marina, you found yourself on the Overseas Highway where cars raced past the Walmarts, Home Depots, and numerous strip malls. Our only reason for stopping was to pick up one more crew, an old friend from the *Eye,* also named Katie, just to make things confusing. Once aboard, we set sail for Key West, where we would wait for our weather window to cross to Cuba.

Our stay in Key West lasted longer than we wished for, as constant northerly winds persisted. You might think that would create excellent conditions for heading due south, but the northerlies created dangerous conditions when arriving at the narrow, dynamited channel of Marina Hemmingway on Cuba's north coast, and often Officials would close the port due to safety concerns. We would have to wait for light easterly or westerly winds.

I became impatient with the waiting game, having too much time to think and stew about things, as sailors often do if they sit in limbo too long, unable to progress towards their final destination. The close quarters were getting the better of all of us, so I set out in search of the place within every community you can be sure to find peace and quiet, the cemetery.

On my way back to the waterfront I ended up on a tour of dead-end roads, which provided many pleasant surprises, including some of the most charming homes of any I'd seen in Florida. There were hundreds of free-range roosters all over the island, which I hadn't known previous to our stop there, and they added an unusual atmosphere. They're protected; it's unlawful to mess with them, and one explanation I'd heard was that it was the last place in America to ban cock fighting, and one day they were all set free. Effie was unaware of State laws, and there may have been a face-off in the confines of the cockpit, where we came home one day to a heap of feathers.

After two weeks, light easterlies were finally in the forecast. Weighing anchor before dawn, we left civilization, as we knew it, behind. It was an uneasy but wonderfully exciting feeling of jumping, eyes-closed, over that ledge into the unknown and trusting the universe; trusting that by experiencing life in a

manner of our own choosing, we might open ourselves
to the unimaginable.

Nine

I remember my first sight of Cuba early on a February morning like it was yesterday; one lonely lighthouse flashed a bright white light about five miles east of Havana. As daylight broke, layers began to emerge as ranges of low hills became hazier with distance. After leaving Key West, we were pushed ever so slightly to the east while crossing that branch of the Gulf Stream, so once across the current, we headed the fifteen miles west to Marina Hemmingway, our final destination about eight miles outside the city. During the crossing, we were circled by an American helicopter a few times, but our Canadian flag was large and convincing enough to not encourage any further contact. I had heard stories of boats being illegally boarded by the United States Coast Guard while in transit to Cuba, and I was hoping this wouldn't happen to us. Shortly before crossing the reef into the marina, we heard *Road to the Isles* on the VHF. As it turned out, they had made the crossing the same day.

Clearing customs and immigration was a circus conducted by two 20-year old boys who had been on the job for two years. *Road to the Isles* cleared relatively quickly, and later admitted that they were becoming concerned that something was wrong when we were still talking to Customs well over an hour later. The first five minutes of the conversation was comprised of the standard questions, such as 'What do you do for work back in Canada,' and 'How long do you plan to stay,' and 'Where in Cuba do you plan to travel.' After that, we were asked where our boyfriends were, told how beautiful we were, and on the back of one of my clearance documents I still have the evidence where they asked me how to say and write *naked* in English.

After leaving the Customs dock, where we were instructed that we'd be required to clear-in and clear-out with the local *Guarda* at all subsequent ports, we moved over to one of the canals of the marina. Once upon a time, Marina Hemmingway was a bustling meeting place for cruisers and racers from all over the world, especially America. Now, it was in a terrible state of disrepair. Crumbled tennis courts, empty swimming pools, dimly lit bathrooms and creepy shower stalls, and an outdoor pub whose seats would never be entirely filled. A couple of seedy security guards who kept an especially watchful eye on *Annie Laurie* and her all-female crew gave one of us unwanted inspiration for inventing a new term: the Cuban Grab.

In a marina built to handle four hundred yachts, the dozen or so there at the peak of the winter cruising season made the whole scene feel a bit sad. American boats no longer allowed by their own country to enter Cuba, though a few did, were largely the reason for the empty piers. After coming all this way, and having gone through so much and with such high hopes of what I was about to experience, my impressions of the country left so much to be desired. After one week in the marina, I was more than ready to jump on the next plane to Canada to get away for a few days.

And so I did.

Now listen, we all have our stories of bad decisions when it comes to dating. In the interest of good taste, I will leave out the details of my personal disasters, but to delete a certain individual from my past would make parts of the coming months difficult to smooth over and properly share the other components of the story. For the consideration of privacy, and to offer a more accurate name to match the character he was, I will call him Jonah[5].

I had flown up to Montreal to visit Jonah, whom I had met in Key West. After a one-week visit that took us from Québec, Vermont, Maine, New York, and back

---

[5] *Jonah*: A person who carries a jinx or brings bad luck to any endeavour.

to Montreal again, he was eager, as an American, to go to the Forbidden Land and see Cuba by boat (not that it would be his first time). We decided to meet again somewhere in western Cuba.

Returning to Havana on an evening flight that put me in the desolate Jose Marti airport in the middle of nowhere at 2:00 AM, I managed to find an older couple willing to share a cab on their way to an all-inclusive resort, and finally arrived back at the boat around 4:00 AM. My sister flew home the same day I flew to Montreal, leaving Katie and Effie boat-sitting for the week. We were all ready at this point to leave the restrictions of the marina and see what the rest of rural Cuba had to offer. Many boats had been waiting for this weather window, and three of us headed west that day. It was the beginning of a great sailing trio consisting of *Annie Laurie*, *Road to the Isles*, and a sloop named *Bacchanal*.

Our first stop after leaving Marina Hemingway was Bahia Honda. Aside from the shack where the Guarda worked from, the only other signs of life was a fishing station on pontoons in one of the sheltered inlets. We stayed long enough to cook supper, go for a swim, and get robbed (the Guarda quietly slipped my stack of Cuban pesos into their pockets, all the money I had exchanged for the duration of our stay) before heading to Cayo Levisa the next day.

One thing I really enjoyed, perhaps too much,

were days when the wind allowed us to haul up the anchor, sail away, and drop anchor in the next harbour without ever laying hands on the engine key. On this particular passage, I recall the wind dying early in the afternoon. We drifted, forward, and backward, and in circles, until the wind picked up again a couple of hours later. In the meantime, *Road to the Isles* and *Bacchanal* motored on well ahead of us, buying the time to dive on a 19th century shipwreck on a shallow reef, that, until now, had been completely off limits by the Cuban government. I wish I had the foresight in those situations to realize what's more important, and where the source of the good memories lie.

Cayo Levisa was the site of an all-inclusive resort (nothing else), and was a very well protected anchorage when a norther strikes. A norther refers to the strong northerly winds that affect the southern United States and Cuba, as well as other surrounding areas, mainly in the wintertime. When the prevailing southeasterly winds began to clock around to the southwest, you knew a front was on the way. You could usually see the line of clouds, and sometimes lightening, as it approached. These winds can potentially blow fifty to sixty knots and can last for days. The worry at times like that was dragging anchor, which I did more than once, as we waited out two back-to-back northers during our six-day stay.

After Cayo Levisa, we began to run into

problems with permission to go ashore. Frustration increased at each port, as all we wanted to do was go explore the country, meet the locals, and be able to stock up on local produce for cooking meals on-board. Instead, they insisted that we only go ashore in ports where we'd be forced to cater to the local restaurants and pay marina fees; places where few or no other amenities, let alone communities, existed.

Once arriving in a small port known as Los Arroyos, all three boats were low on supplies (and fresh drinking water), so we went ashore in search of a market. The Guarda told us *no* at first, but after some insisting, he made a phone call to his boss in Havana, and we were then allowed ashore for one hour, so long as one of the Guarda could follow us around. Being Monday, the market was closed, so we started asking people on the street if they had any food in their gardens they'd like to sell. One man was especially helpful, toting his bottle of white rum under one arm, speaking gibberish (or Spanish, at this point I wouldn't be able to tell the difference) as he stumbled into a dozen houses and tried, in his language, to say we needed food. They weren't allowed to accept money from tourists, so we were careful to pass over a few pesos when it appeared the ever-present *policia* weren't looking. After finding some bananas and green tomatoes, we were escorted back to the boat, precisely one hour later.

Communication was extremely difficult, expensive, and sporadic in Cuba, and the nature of sailing is uncertainty of plans, so trying to figure out where Jonah could connect with us was complicated. As the date approached when he was due to arrive in Havana, the best I could do was to say I would try to make it to Maria La Gorda the day of his flight (the first stop on the south coast of Cuba after rounding the western cape), and he could swim out to the boat when he got there. That day arrived, and I was in a place called Los Morros, the last stop on the north coast.

Katie and I joined our friends from *Bacchanal*, who had rented a car in Los Morros to drive the two hours to Pinar Del Rio, the nearest city, where supplies and access to Internet (with valid foreign passport) could be found. On the way, we drove to Maria La Gorda, hoping to find him, or maybe his tent pitched on the beach somewhere. I left a note at the main desk of the diving resort, where I figured he would stop in on arrival. I explained how I was at a 'marina' on the north coast (the marina was little more than a long concrete dock, with a restaurant containing four tables, and a shower facility that consisted of a hole in the wall with a plastic pipe that spewed cold water out the side), and how an approaching norther would force us to move to a safe anchorage at Cayos de la Lena by evening. The anchorage, five miles away from the marina, was completely inaccessible by land, being in the middle of what I imagine was miles of mangroves. So, if I didn't find him by sunset, then it may have been a few days before I'd be able to make contact with him again.

We continued on the long, long drive to Pinar Del Rio, and I figured I might be able to check his whereabouts by email shortly. I was sitting in the front seat of the rental car, closely watching every car, truck, bus, and horse-driven wagon that passed by, hoping to intercept him on his way to Maria La Gorda. But I kept losing concentration, and became discouraged at the thought that his car had passed while I was zoned-out and daydreaming. Then in the distance up ahead, I saw a guy wearing a familiar rugby shirt, standing next to a broken-down taxi, a 1948 Chevy. We had found him. What a great bit of luck.

At least that's how I saw it at the time.

Ten

After finding Jonah by the roadside, we eventually made our way back to Los Morros, arriving around 4:00 PM. We were told the immigration officer would be a little while getting there, and that Jonah could not be officially signed onto the boat until he arrived. As I mentioned, there was a strong front forecast to move through the area that evening, and persist for as long as three days. We waited and waited for this officer to come and do the necessary paperwork, all the while watching the lightning on the horizon get closer. The winds began to freshen and were soon blowing twenty-five knots from the northwest. I was beginning to get angry, because the safety of the boat was at stake and the longer we waited, the harder it would be to get off the concrete dock we were getting blown against, and the longer and more uncomfortable it would be to motor through choppy seas to the safe anchorage five miles away.

At 8:00 PM, one of the marina workers informed us the immigration officer would be arriving shortly, having completed an errand of dropping off groceries from Pinar Del Rio to the marina restaurant (apparently no job was too big or too small for government officials). Unfortunately by that point it was neither here nor there, as the boss in Havana who would have to give final permission to allow Jonah on board had gone home for the day at 5:00 PM. For Jonah to be signed on the next day, both 'Captain and Vessel' had to be dockside to meet with Immigration at 8:00 AM. So what choice did I have? Leave Jonah at the dock with no place to stay and come back a few days later? In my mind, that wasn't an option. In Jonah's mind, it was the *only* option, and he was adamant that I go, and we'd sort everything out in a few days. My final decision though was to stay dockside through the storm and hope to clear Immigration as early as possible in the morning before getting the hell out of there.

We had an extensive discussion with a young dissident who was in charge of the marina that night. He had full empathy for our situation, but explained the position I'd be putting all the employees in if I were to ignore their rules and take off with Jonah to the anchorage (which I was entirely prepared to do as soon as I caught the slightest whiff of hassle, but Jonah refused). The marina employees would be held responsible, they would all face being fired and would lose their $20/month, and in some cases $10/month. This young fellow went out of his way to get permission that provided Jonah with a one-night pass to stay on board the boat, provided I stay at the marina until morning. It all seemed so preposterous, coming from a free country. Why should it be such a circus to allow a friend to stay overnight on my own private boat? What right did they have to tell us *no,* and to put me in the position where I was forced to decide between Jonah and the safety of my boat?

Having resigned ourselves to the fact that we weren't going anywhere, we pulled out what was to be our last bottle of Cuban rum, and passed it around while chatting with a couple of local fishermen, as we watched the lightning show on the distant horizon.

It was a long, sleepless night, much of which saw Katie, Jonah and I on deck, kicking the fenders back between the boat and the concrete dock, as they constantly popped out of place as the boat bucked violently in the swell. I had extra dock lines tied to various cleats across the dock, and whenever one would break, I'd throw on another one, and do the best to splice the broken one as quickly as possible. I had made matters worse for myself by having more than my share of the bottle of rum, but after dealing with that over the port side, I eventually came to my own peace with the situation. I was actually in pretty good spirits as I leaned against the cabin in the pouring cold rain at 4:00 AM with one foot ready to kick the next fender that popped out of place.

In true Cuban style, when 8:00 AM rolled around, with no further ado and Jonah below half asleep, his passport was handed over and we were told we could leave. They didn't need to come aboard, or speak to Jonah, or even see him, and I never did see Immigration. We got ready to cast off, and the fishermen and the dissident were there to see us off.

Three hours later we were reunited with *Road to the Isles* and *Bacchanal* in Cayos de la Lena. We sailed under a reefed main around the mangroves and into the narrow canal, rounded up into the wind and dropped the hook, congratulated by the cheers of our friends. What a completely unnecessary farce it had been. I feel sorry for the hopeful sailors I've since encountered, with their own dreams of Cuba, as I cannot hold back my contempt for the place. And this incident would not mark the end of *Annie Laurie's* troubles in Cuba.

Without the company of other boats, I'm afraid my short trip along the north coast of Cuba would have few redeeming qualities. Having originally planned to go as far as Cienfuegos on the south coast, by the time I reached Los Morros, the western tip of Cuba, as alluring as the diving and natural wonders of the apparently fairer coast seemed, I was *more* than ready to bail. *Bacchanal* was bound for Isla Mujeres,

Mexico, and after some thought and discussion I decided we would follow.

Difficulties with officials and paperwork persisted to the bitter end as we tried to clear out of Los Morros. Clearing with the Guarda always involved bringing the Guarda aboard, having them search the boat, sign my cruising permit, check our passports, and occasionally take our wallets or personal items as souvenirs. As the hours wore on, waiting for our clearance, I became more uptight about making it to Mexico before dark the following day. Only having one large-scale chart of part of the Mexican coast and a digital photograph of a sketch from a cruising guide belonging to our Australian friends, I was definitely keen on getting through the reef with daylight on my side. Sure, I could have been a little better prepared, but the hold-up on the Cuban end contributed to one final kick in the shins for which I will always hold Cuban Immigration somewhat accountable.

§§§

It wasn't until after 3:00 PM that we were finally able to make tracks to Isla Mujeres, Mexico. This resulted in a sunset arrival at the edge of the reef skirting the island, and as we rounded it's northern point, we hoped we had cleared the most precarious portion of our voyage. We might have if Mexico paid any attention to their aids to navigation, and adjusted them as necessary when sandy bottoms would shift, and channels would become shoal, and shoals channels. As we coasted southward after dark, with a three-foot following sea, I could clearly see we were well within the buoys that marked the channel. If it were daylight, I easily could have seen the growing beach ahead as well. I detected a preliminary nudge, which Jonah insisted was just the natural motion of the boat in these seas. I knew we were on the verge of hitting bottom, and quickly radioed my friends on *Bacchanal* in the hopes they could somehow tell me whether I was more likely to be on the verge of hitting the beach side of the channel, or the shoal side. When I informed them I could see the tiki bar three hundred feet to my left, they were certain I was going for the beach. It was already too late.

Doug was on the scene within minutes in his dinghy, leaving Marissa aboard *Bacchanal* to radio surrounding boats to solicit the assistance I urgently needed. I was trying desperately to go back the way I came by putting the engine in reverse, but with three-foot waves and a good wind on my stern, *Annie Laurie* continued forward. About ten minutes passed before Marissa and three men in a dinghy from boats in the anchorage came out to help. By this point, the boat was jammed so far onto the beach, she sat in little more than four feet of water. With every successive wave, she was repeatedly picked up and smashed down, and my blood still runs cold every time I recall that feeling and sound. The entire boat would crack and shudder, the masts springing back and forth violently. I could tell by the look in Doug's eyes he felt my pain, and he reassured me everything was going to be okay.

As much as I would like to say how *good* everyone was throughout the ensuing two-hour ordeal, it was the work of just two that would get me out of this dilemma. I sat back in amazement as four men argued and schemed and theorized, ignoring every word the *wife* of the Captain of *Annie Laurie* (as I had quickly been sized up to be) was calmly trying to request they do. I failed miserably that day to assert any authority that might have lessened the duration of which she banged and smashed on what might as well have been concrete. Doug and Marissa recognized what was going on with the Captain's Meeting on the quarterdeck, when there really was no time to talk, and the only option we had was simple and obvious. They had brought a spare anchor from *Bacchanal*, and passing me the end of the anchor line, they motored out into the darkness to drop the anchor as far from my stern as the line allowed. With the salvage tactic decided and underway, the men now jumped in to help take turns cranking on the winch, with the engine in reverse, to back her off the beach.

It was an agonizing two hours of dropping

anchors and winching her back before she was finally into deeper water. Doug offered to guide us into the inner anchorage that night, but I was so emotionally exhausted, I just couldn't face it. I opted to stay in the channel for the night. On top of this, Jonah had excused himself from the difficult chore of cranking the winch early on, claiming to have pulled a muscle in his shoulder, and now that we were safely at anchor and assistance had gone home, he was curled up like a child looking for comfort. Where was mine? I would have been better off alone at this point; even Effie was always tuned in to my distresses and would have been there for me, but she disagreed with my choice in men this time, and she remained aloof. A little sidebar I like to recall as a testament to her intelligence: One month later, after learning of infidelity number two (fool me once shame on you, fool me twice, shame on me) Jonah came aboard to apologize. She sat at his feet, curiously scanning his face, before lunging upward and swinging her claws across his lips and nose; it took twenty minutes to stop the bleeding. That's my girl.

I should have stuck to my guns when, a few days later, I said I wasn't going anywhere until he packed his bags and was on a bus back to America. There were so many strange notions going through my mind those days, as I felt I was to blame for never having made a relationship really *work.* I know there were times, despite everything that seems so obvious now, that we were somehow destined for each other, if I was only tolerant of his misbehaviour and could accept him for who he was, and if I could only smarten up and see how selfishly I'd been living. Without any close friends to confide in, it was very difficult to see things for what they were, and, in fact, to think rationally at all. My world had become very, very small, and my mind had become my own worst enemy. Unfortunately, I needed crew to make the four-day sail back to Key West, and wasn't sure I would find anyone in Mexico, and so, he stayed. After five *very* long weeks of living at anchor on a tiny boat and hating each other to the core, we finally had our weather to return to the States. Upon stepping outside after clearing Customs, I said we were through.

If only I was better at keeping my word.

Eleven

Key West was to become my home for the next three months. I found my niche amongst a small community of young live-aboard sailors, and even found some part-time work with a local entrepreneur, maintaining his fleet of rental bicycles across the island. I worked until I could afford a haul-out for *Annie Laurie.* The warm waters in this area are known to harbour teredo worms, which can do extensive damage to wooden boats. It wouldn't hurt to get another coat of bottom paint on the hull.

In the days leading up to the haul-out, I tried to get a head start at cleaning the bottom growth off the hull. I couldn't explain why, but since arriving in Key West, I'd developed an irrational fear of the water. I'd grown up by the sea, swimming in icy waters in both Nova Scotia and Prince Edward Island. I'd swam alongside barracuda in the Caribbean and jumped into unfamiliar and frigid black waters that seemed

125

bottomless from the edge of the rocks on the Isle of Mull in Scotland. But when I got into the warm, clear waters in Key West, I panicked. Breathing became difficult, and any string of seaweed slipping across the back of my neck or any distant splash caused me to race to the front of the boat where I could grab onto the head rig and pull myself out of the water, if only to hang above the surface for a minute to regain my composure.

It was a whole other challenge to then put my head under the water. I found something unsettling about seeing my boat from underwater, how she appeared to be suspended effortlessly in mid-air. I tried not to let my eyes wander from the job at hand; I didn't want to see the flow of the sea grass growing on the bottom, just a few feet deeper than the keel. I worked my way from stern to bow, scrubbing and occasionally slicing my hands on barnacles as I braced myself away from the side, until a passing boat tossed me a glove (it seemed they'd done this before). The cuts stung in the salt water, but I was less worried about the pain than what the blood might have been attracting. As I completed the upper portion of the port side, I approached the bow and allowed my eyes to drift forward to my mooring chain, visually following it down to the bottom. It was the first time I had seen what was responsible for holding my boat in place. Not surprisingly, it was a sunken boat; but not just any boat. It was a *wooden* boat. No seaweed or splashing fish or hammerhead shark could have made me clamber out of the water any faster. Perhaps you have to be a wooden boat owner to sympathize with such a reaction, but I felt like I'd seen a dead body. In that moment, I decided my prep-work was sufficient.

I set my alarm for a 5:00 AM wake-up on Thursday, and I made my way to my 8:00 AM appointment. I was required to sign a waiver to haul in this yard (for a couple of reasons) so if anything were to go wrong, I might have been looking for a new hobby, house, and mode of transportation. I got a bit carried away in my thoughts of impending doom, but it all went off without a hitch. She was placed in her spot in the yard, lowered onto supporting blocks so the weight of the boat was on the keel, and jack stands were placed on either side for added stability.

I had booked to haul her 8:00 AM Thursday and to 'splash' her at 4:00 PM Friday (as usual, I was on a tight budget). I went into high gear, not wanting to waste a precious minute. I had my spotlight and headlamp and spare batteries on hand, fully intending to work well into the night. But not long after I began to scrape and scrub the remaining growth on the bottom, the yard manager offered for me to stay the weekend and splash at 4:00 PM Monday, at no additional cost ('must be great having boobs', many of the male boat owners at the yard commented). I took him up on the offer, of course. But rather than taking it easy, I extended my list of things-to-do and decided to finally face a challenge that had been a source of constant worry. I had good reason to believe that many of the fasteners holding the planks to the frames were severely degraded. If any of them let go, then I would probably have a sprung plank on my hands. This was always going through my mind when I was out in any sort of unsettled weather, especially while off Cape Fear the year before.

So my solution, until Jonah's father simplified the whole dilemma and proposed a better one, was to replace every nut and bolt, most of which were buried behind different parts of the interior construction of the boat. Bill suggested using bronze screws to reinforce each plank end. That way, it could all be done from the outside of the hull. Brilliant. I bought a box of silicon bronze screws, and Bill helped with drill-bits and counter-sinks, and wooden plugs that would cover the screws once they were in place. Less than eight hours from when I began, I had drilled, screwed, plugged, and painted over sixty new holes below the waterline. I never thought myself able to do such a thing even a week earlier, not considering my experience sufficient to drill holes in the most important component of the boat, but with some good advice, the job was done.

There were a few other things I had to deal with while she was high and dry. She was missing bottom paint in a few places, having been chafed off by the anchor chain in a storm. There were sacrificial zincs that needed replacing (zincs are attached to metal below the waterline, like the propeller shaft, and the metal brackets that hold the rudder, so the electrolysis attacks the zincs first). I had a moderate leak in the stern that I wanted to caulk, and the bronze propeller needed to be scraped of its community of barnacles.

Once the boat was on the hard, I preferred to bike back to Key West to Jonah's parents place and have a comfortable (air-conditioned) room before going all-out during daylight hours. Effie took the opportunity to make an escape while unattended one night. She had jumped the six or so feet onto a sawhorse and took off into the night. Once free, I thought she'd be dazzled by the shore life and swooning over tomcats, so I didn't hold out a lot of hope of finding her. Then I thought about what a lackluster ending to her story that would be; having sailed all the way from Nova Scotia, to Cuba, and Mexico, and back again, in fair seas and through storms, then to just disappear in a boatyard, never to be heard from again? I didn't like the sounds of that, and I started wishing she'd just come home.

A big part of the whole yard experience for me was the presence of another wooden boat, a Rosborough designed schooner built in Nova Scotia, no less. Matthew was overseeing the cold moulding[6] of the hull of *Compass Rose*. He had a lot of wooden boat experience, so was very helpful on a daily basis, providing me with some of the larger tools I required but didn't carry aboard, and was always offering welcomed input. Most evenings I went over and had dinner and wine with him and his work crew. It was my favourite part of the day.

On the final day, after the boat had been launched and was tied far down the dock (*not* where Effie had left her) I was at *Compass Rose,* saying goodbye. There were witnesses who said Effie had returned to where the boat had been, and was curled up next to my bike. She was gone by the time I returned.

I decided to take a spin on my bike around the yard and surrounding vacant properties, calling her name into the trees and in the direction of other boats upon which she may have stowed away. It wasn't long before I was met with one long continuous *meow* as she trotted along the fence trying to find a gap to get through. Her apparent lover followed her to a certain point, then, realizing I had more of a hold on her than he did, he gave up the chase, watching as I dropped her into my bike basket and peddled to the boat. As Effie looked longingly back at her Tom, I reassured her she deserved much better, if he let her get away *that* easily.

So with Effie home, and the boat in the water, I

---

[6] A process by which a wooden boat in hopeless condition is given new life by coating the hull in fiberglass.

was prepared to sail back to Key West, just in time for the beginning of the Atlantic hurricane season.

§§§

One day before the official start of hurricane season, the first named storm was announced, Tropical Storm Arthur. For a storm to be named, it must reach a minimum of tropical storm status, which is defined by sustained winds of 34 knots or higher. The names are dealt out in alphabetical order and taken from a predetermined list. It just so happened that the name chosen for when the letter 'L' was up to bat that year was Laura. I contemplated the possible irony of a Hurricane Laura hitting Key West while I was anchored in this very Hurricane-prone corner of the country.

The beginning of the hurricane season marked the end of Hurricane Awareness Week, which I followed with keen interest. I anticipated that I would receive more information than I really wanted, giving me more reasons to worry by providing me with more scenarios of just how bad things could really become. It was just the opposite. I learned that it had been over a hundred years since the last hurricane of Category 3 (sustained winds of ninety-six knots) or higher had hit Key West. The last Category 5 (sustained winds of a hundred and thirty-five knots or more) was in 1846. The categories are 1 to 5; 1 being the weakest, and 5 being something you never want to experience. Statistically speaking, Key West is more likely to be hit by a hurricane than other areas of the southern United States, but when it *is* struck, it's more likely to experience a hurricane of lesser severity.

Cuba actually deserves some thanks for this fact. Because of its landmass, it can take a lot of the steam out of a hurricane before it makes its way to the Keys. To sustain themselves, as well as to increase in intensity, hurricanes require the heat and moisture of the warm sea surface beneath them. So, a relatively weak storm hitting the Keys can carry on to track offshore and up the coast, increasing in strength along the way and thus be able to do far greater damage to the remainder of the east coast United States.

I had a few options for riding out the inevitable storms and felt my plans were somewhat in place after taking a survey of many locals who had dealt with the threat of hurricanes for years.

Up to a certain wind velocity, I felt I would be safe on my mooring, which was very strong. The worst case scenario in that situation would be to be struck by another boat that had broken free of its mooring, or dragged its anchor. Anything over sixty-five knots I wanted to consider one of two other options. Going dockside to a floating dock was one. Key West Bight was well protected from the winds and waves, having a small entrance, and being surrounded by the town on three sides and by a partial breakwater on the fourth. However, one of the most dangerous aspects of a hurricane is in fact *not* the high winds and waves, but the accompanying storm surge. A storm surge is a significant and fast increase in the sea level caused partly by the high winds of a hurricane, and partly by how fast the atmospheric pressure drops in the vicinity of the low-pressure center. A storm surge can have disastrous effects if water levels cause the floating docks to rise higher than the long posts that are meant to keep them in place. At that point, the whole system would come undone and it would then become perfectly conceivable that my boat could end up two blocks away in Jonah's back yard. A friend in the anchorage lost his previous boat from a floating dock in this manner during Hurricane Wilma a few years earlier, only to have it spotted by the Coast Guard off the coast of Miami a week later, and two hundred miles away.

Option number two was a much more traditional method of procuring the safety of the boat. It involved seeking out an area of mangroves (low, stout bushes that are the first form of plant life to stick their heads above the water, as islands form out of coral reefs). Where these bushes border narrow canals, I could make the boat as a spider in a web, sending lines off in a dozen directions to the sturdy roots of the mangroves. One such area outside Key West was Navy property, used at one time as a home for submarines. The Navy was more than happy to lift their restrictions in the case of hurricanes and let private boaters run for safety. There were marinas whose moral responsibility was not aligned with that of the Navy, and some of them actually *increased* their rates in the event of a hurricane. No, this wasn't Provincetown.

The weather, and more specifically the winds, had been and would continue to be responsible for the direction my life took. When I reflected on how far I'd come, and where I thought I'd be by now (just completing my circumnavigation of Cuba) I saw how those winds had decided where I would go, if I would go, how far I would get, and who would accompany me. If I had met my goal of Christmas in Cuba sipping on mojitos, many things that defined my life now would be much different. The wind may not explain *why* it had decided all these various fates, but living this way, knowing it was nature that had *Annie Laurie* on its puppet strings, helped me to trust its path.

Twelve

For those who know me well, you know about my fishing shack. It's on the Atlantic coast of Nova Scotia, where the icy rollers crash into the granite much of the year, and the craggy trees cling to life, rooted in the ice-formed cracks of their supporting rocks. It's a crooked one-room shack with multi-paned windows looking onto that every-changing and terrifying sea, from the comfort of a hundred-year-old building that has stood the test of the elements and time. There is a Franklin cast-iron stove in the corner, burning lumber cut by my own hands, and warming the kettle for my Earl Grey tea. Wooden walls, wooden floors, with every imperfection, containing knots that display many works of art, like the bleeding heart that hung above my head in my childhood bunk-bed at the family cottage. And, naturally, no inner ceiling to mask the sound of the tapping rain on the roof.

Weathered cedar shingles on the outer walls, a

simple stovepipe, and the backyard landscape is a forest of my own, subtly divided by a small dirt road that is rarely used by more than a bicycle. Blueberries, raspberries, and strawberries grow wild in the scrubby bushes in the summer, and nothing grows in winter besides the night. My home library becomes ever more populated in these times, and I'm content in knowing that the changing seasons bring their own discoveries, that nothing is forever, and there is a reason for absolutely everything.

Every sailor has their alternative dream, what they'd be doing if they were home; what they'd be doing if the boat didn't consume every reserve of energy, and every copper penny passed under the table or over. This is *my* dream, and some nights, following little more than a couple of lonely days, it was almost strong enough to draw me home. No crew, no autopilot, and two to three weeks at sea in my own company, yet it was a feeling strong enough to make that possibility seem rational. But, alas, I knew I wouldn't go, at least not at this point. Timing was wrong. This fishing shack had existed in my imagination long before I ever stepped foot on a sailboat, and the possibility of making it a reality wasn't about to disappear in the passing of one more summer, autumn, and winter.

Thirteen

Adventures continued to arise, despite *Annie Laurie* being bound to the Key West anchorage for a few months. The 1925 schooner *Hindu*, whose ownership had been under dispute in recent months, had just been returned to her rightful owner, Foggy, as he's known to friends. To avoid further difficulty in getting the boat underway to Provincetown, Massachusetts, where Foggy had been intending all along to take her for the summer months that year, he decided to get the boat out of Key West promptly and take her to an undisclosed location to have her prepared for the rest of the northward journey. We had to act fast when the 'other' owner finally stepped off the boat after a three-hour standoff. Despite having received an injunction that morning banning him from the vessel, he refused to leave, and he paced the deck, swinging and occasionally striking a large wooden mallet normally used for firing the ships ceremonial canon, while yelling at Foggy, myself, and two other crew to get off *his* boat. When he was informed the Key West Police and County Sheriff were on their way, he decided to avoid further embarrassment (a crowd was beginning to form) and he quietly stepped off the boat. We cast off the lines and started motoring away; Foggy, Finbar, Jonathan and myself.

Finbar, a good friend of Foggy's, was introduced to me as Admiral of the Conch Republic Navy. The Conch Republic was established when the Florida Keys seceded from the United States in 1982 in response to a United States Border Patrol Blockade setup on highway U.S. 1 just north of the Florida Keys. This effectively isolated Keys inhabitants from the U.S. mainland since the blockade was on the only road to and from the mainland. There was a protest, and the Mayor of Key West, along with a few other Conchs (as Key West locals are known), went to Federal court in Miami to seek an injunction to stop the blockade, but to no avail. Upon leaving the Federal Court House, the mayor announced to the world by way of TV crews and reporters, "Tomorrow at noon, the Florida Keys will secede from the Union!"

At noon the following day, at Mallory Square in Key West, the mayor read the proclamation of secession and announced that the Conch Republic was an independent nation separate from the United States, then symbolically began the Conch Republic's Civil Rebellion by breaking a loaf of stale Cuban bread over the head of a man dressed in a U.S. Navy uniform. After one minute of rebellion, the mayor, now Prime Minister, turned to the Admiral in charge of the Navy Base at Key West, and surrendered to the Union Forces, and demanded one billion dollars in war relief to rebuild the nation after the long Federal siege.

So, as one might imagine, Finbar, the Admiral of the only all-sail Navy fleet in the world, and organizer of the annual re-creation of the Great Sea Battle (which, of course, never really happened), is quite the character.

We sailed through the night, up the Florida Keys and out into the Gulf Stream, and eventually made our way to a top-secret marina. I had a lot on my mind during the brief voyage as I listened to the details of an ownership dispute between two individuals who used to be good friends. I could relate the stories to recent circumstances in my own life, and it gave me a lot to think about, how miscommunications and misunderstandings can lead to so much unnecessary confusion and strife in one's life, and how friendships can so easily, and not so easily, slip away.

We can, to an extent, decide whom we want to bring into our lives, but we can't decide who will choose to keep us in theirs. Most of us often see things the way *we* want to see them, but it would be enlightening to keep our minds open enough to at least contemplate another perspective. By ignoring our own character flaws and simply finding another distraction to keep us from facing what prevents us from becoming deeper and more empathetic individuals, we are ultimately delaying our own happiness. We can only work on our own issues and try to improve on the faults that others point out to us, or, if we're lucky enough, ones which we manage to recognize ourselves through our own mistakes. Others may not share our ideals in morality, loyalty, or any other important criteria that define a friendship, but to try to affect a change in their behaviour is ultimately fruitless, as many will unwittingly choose to live in blind disagreement and self-justification.

There's no time like the present to face these flaws that we *all* possess, and the more a person avoids doing this, the further and further they will find themselves from ever being truly satisfied in their lives, and for that matter, sincerely loved.

Some people will spend the rest of their lives running from themselves, and others will find themselves through running. Speaking for myself, a change of scenery can help to break a bad cycle of stagnant behaviour and thoughts. That short voyage on the Hindu was a wake-up call; I felt refreshed, and finally realized that although I loved Key West and my Conch parents and *most* of the people I'd met, I had been there too long.

Effie and I departed Key West the following Tuesday, Canada Day, well before the break of dawn. Destination: east. It was all I knew of my future at that moment, and I was entirely tranquil in my decision to go.

§§§

Hindu having left their dock vacant and well on their way to Provincetown, I was able, as I had in P-town, to tie up at their designated wharf for a while. I was able to top-up on water and gather groceries as well as bring down all my personal items that had gradually accumulated at Jonah's parents house. I had one oar stolen my last day in the anchorage (who steals *one* oar?) so being able to come dockside greatly simplified and sped up the process of getting out of town.

While tying up all the loose ends, I suddenly became very aware of everything I'd been taking for granted. I would miss rollerblading along Smathers Beach, having hollering conversations with my anchorage neighbour Jonathon from his nearby boat, and would even miss greeting the homeless drunks of Simonton Beach (who would never ask for money; they cut to the chase and always asked for beer, or sometimes specific mixed cocktails). I'd miss biking around on Jonah's 'Conch cruiser', which I painted white with red maple leaves to reflect my nationality. He hadn't been in Key West long enough recently to notice, but I was sure he'd find the humour in the incessant "Canadian, eh? Canadian, eh? Canadian, eh?" which accompanied any bike ride I'd taken through a busy part of town. I would miss the very social Tuesday night poker games hosted by Jonah's dad, hours of great conversation with his mom, and reading the Citizen's Voice over a cup of Bustelo coffee in the hours before dawn.

The crew of the schooner *Western Union*, all having an appreciation for wooden boats, came over and introduced themselves that final night, and I regret that I hadn't met one of them in particular sooner. To think we lived within a short boat ride of one another, and we met only long enough to say hello, share a few glasses of wine, and say goodbye. Life's like that. I couldn't help but wonder if I had been more decisive and less passive with whom I chose to spend my time, if something more meaningful and true may have arose. Hindsight is twenty-twenty, and clarity was abundant once I found myself out of the Jonah situation. I couldn't dwell on what may have been; I could only promise myself I wouldn't make the same mistakes again. I hoped I had acquired the tools to become a much better judge of men, and people in general.

It became helpful at this point to remind myself

of all the things I *wouldn't* miss about Key West. The swarms of mosquitoes, rowing against 2 knots of current to get ashore, the way my Popsicle would start to drip before I got it out of the plastic, or the feeling of having a propane torch held to my face as I rowed across the harbour in little or no wind under a sun that seemed to ignore any ozone barrier. There were a few good reasons to stay in Key West, but many better ones to leave. It was once again time to trust the universe, and welcome uncertainty.

§§§

My first stop after leaving Key West was Bahia Honda. I had missed this anchorage on my way down in January, instead stopping at Marathon. I had a certain image of what the Florida Keys would be like before I arrived; long white sandy beaches, wading out to coral reefs to snorkel among exotic fish, palm trees swaying in the breeze, and crystal-clear turquoise water. That is what I finally found when I dropped the hook at Bahia Honda.

There was a strong current running in the anchorage, and being minus one oar, I opted not to bother launching *James* off the stern, knowing I probably couldn't paddle fast enough to get to shore before I got sucked out under the retired Flagler Railroad Bridge and out to sea. Instead, I pulled out my flippers and snorkel and put my camera in a waterproof case and swam in.

I wanted to stay much longer in Bahia Honda, but after a swim and making *Annie Laurie* the subject of a photo-shoot, the clock was approaching noon and I knew I had to leave. I still had many miles of heading due east ahead of me, and the winds were unrelentingly east this time of year, so the best I could hope for was to motor against the winds while they were still relatively light. The forecast at the time gave me eight more hours of relatively easy motoring before reaching the corner where I could start heading north.

That day I didn't make it as far as I had hoped, and I found myself with darkness falling and no good place to drop my anchor. With the winds increasing to twenty knots from the east, I had no place to hide, and the sea floor was either coral or sea grass (coral not an option for anchoring, and sea grass provided poor holding). I was hoping to find a sandy spot, because my Bruce anchor set best in sand or mud. I had slowed down, and was up on the bow trying to look ahead for that token bit of sand, when out of nowhere appeared a high-speed boat with four officials aboard. It was United States Customs and Border Patrol. Great, just in time to ask them for local knowledge on where to anchor. It seemed wise to let them get their business out of the way first, the young guy at the helm looking angry, like his training had taught him to intimidate no matter what the situation. The older guy in charge though was level headed and reasonable, and could even be described as overly friendly. I swear he was French Canadian.

"How many abcard?" he asked.

"Just us," as I pointed to Effie.

The look of surprise, which I'd become accustomed to as a woman sailing alone, told me that none of this was going to be a problem. The guy at the helm, staying on task, demanded, "Port side or starboard side boarding, Sir?" and the fellow I was speaking with waved his hand at him to tell him to be quiet. They weren't going to board a vessel with a single girl aboard. He asked if I had a cruising permit, I said yes. He asked if it was handy, and when I said no, but that it was valid until November, he took my word for it. He asked where I was from, how long I'd been sailing, what I did for a living back home, and if I'd sailed all this way by myself. He commented on how friendly Effie was, and that normally animals on boats were terrified of their two 250 horsepower engines, and usually run below. She stood by the rail, wondering if they were going to bring their boat close enough so she could jump and have some new territory to explore.

Sufficiently satisfied I wasn't running drugs or smuggling Cubans, they wished me luck and gave advice on where to anchor, which involved winding through a shallow creek with unlit marks. They had held me up just long enough for the sun to drop below the horizon, so I opted to anchor just where they had stopped me. I knew I'd drag anchor all night, so I just made sure I had plenty of room to drag, and decided I'd wake up every half hour through the night to check my position. That was just a necessary fact, and I didn't care because I knew sleep was going to be impossible regardless. The boat rolled and bucked in the swell all night. At the first sign of dawn, I got ready to go, and wondered what on God's green earth was more difficult than hauling, by hand, a thirty-three pound anchor and fifty feet of chain from fifteen feet of water in twenty knots of wind and three-foot swells after a sleepless night and before my morning coffee, with no one there to sympathize with my complaints.

I left the VHF on the weather station all day as they gave continuous updates on the position and movement of a massive thunderstorm moving across north Key Largo, packing sixty-knot winds, torrential rains that would limit visibility to an eighth of a mile, hail the size of pennies, and the risk of 'frequent deadly lightning strikes', as they put it. These were not comforting words when you're sailing through the narrowest part of the reef (less than a quarter mile wide) and you're the tallest thing in sight. By this time, I was sailing north, so the wind was sufficiently from behind to allow me to sail without the engine running. Wanting to beat this storm, I fired up the engine once more, and averaged seven knots the rest of the way to Key Biscayne. The storm fell behind, and I felt I'd made a good decision, despite the current price of diesel.

Motoring through the final channel, tired from stress and no sleep the night before, and dehydrated from sunburn, I clenched my teeth and crossed my fingers as I crossed over five-foot charted depths of coral heads. I had woven through them before when I left Key Biscayne months ago, but the seas had been calm, and my mind was sharp enough to follow the incremental changes on my hand-held GPS. I wasn't feeling so sharp now, and found myself just hoping for the best. I made educated guesses at my position, and did my best to read the color of the water, diverting away from the whiter shades and trying to stay over the green (which I assumed to be seagrass). What can I say. It worked.

While in Key Biscayne, I received an offer from an elementary school friend, Brian, to sail with him from Vancouver to Alaska. Friends of friends offered to keep an eye on *Annie Laurie* for the summer season at their dock in northern Florida, and Brian assured me Effie would be safe to accompany us, as he'd stopped eating cats after *Alf* was cancelled.

Finally, I had a plan.

Part Three

We must always change, renew, rejuvenate
ourselves; otherwise we harden.

Johann Wolfgang von Goethe

Fourteen

Now thousands of miles from *Annie Laurie,* the warm sandy beaches had turned to towering forested mountains, shrouded in cold rains and specked with waterfalls. Two-ton logs replaced intense squalls and lightening storms as the primary navigational hazard. Shallow coral and sandy bottoms became fathomless, and turquoise waters were still turquoise, but twenty degrees colder, glacial runoff being their source.

I was now aboard Brian's thirty-foot sloop *Nirmala* in Squamish, British Columbia. Although we technically knew each other since kindergarten, I had seen Brian only once since graduating from high school. And to be completely honest, the only reason I knew we went to high school together was his photo in the high school yearbook. I had no clear memory of seeing him in the school hallways since junior high. Online social networking had recently informed us that we'd been living parallel lives on opposite coasts. He had moved to the Pacific and bought his sailboat to live aboard around the same time I found *Annie Laurie* on the Atlantic. Now, we could get to know one another as adults.

I was thrilled to be back in Canada. Within days of arriving, we set out on our first shake-down sail to Gibsons, a small town on the Sunshine Coast only accessible by water. In the days to follow, we did a brief tour of Vancouver Island, exploring Salt Spring Island, Sydney, and Victoria, before returning to Squamish, where we settled down to the important task of seriously thinking through the journey we were about to embark on, and making proper provisions to prepare *Nirmala* for a passage to Alaska.

§§§

By late August, we departed Squamish, northward bound. Solid southeasterly breezes, uncharacteristic of the area that time of year, helped us to northern Vancouver Island via the Inside Passage with little need for the motor. Our first stop, Smugglers Cove, was a popular and cozy nook with an entrance barely fifty feet wide, yet with sixty feet of depth. Young families, mostly on small sailboats, surrounded us, out for one last family trip before sending the kids back to school for the autumn.

We had early starts each day to take advantage

of the great wind while it lasted, and by mid-afternoon on our second day underway from Squamish, we were close to Cortes Island, carrying a reefed main in gale force winds. We rounded one final rocky ledge before making our approach to the gorge, where safe harbour would be found.

The gorge entrance itself was fully exposed to the wind and swells, and had its own background of swirls and whirlpools. The sound of the wind in the rigging had the effect of making conditions seem far worse than they actually were, so I tried to imagine complete silence, and suddenly none of it seemed so intense. I couldn't get used to the fact that I was no longer on my own boat, and I frequently felt the same stress and responsibility on board *Nirmala* as I did on *Annie Laurie.* Brian, I was learning, could appear nonchalant during moments that seemed, to me, to be marginally perilous. He pointed out the petroglyphs on the gorge wall as we transited the narrowest point of the entrance, when it seemed we barely had control of the tiller. I wondered how I could feel so stressed when it was his boat, and he didn't appear remotely concerned.

Once inside the harbour, we eventually found a spot protected from the gale-force winds outside. About ten minutes after setting the anchor and putting the kettle on for tea, driving rains began, along with frantic cries and looks of desperation from Effie.

I had noticed she had been putting on a little

weight in the last two months, but I thought she was just 'filling out' as she approached her first birthday. Within minutes, two tiny paws appeared, and with it, confirmation that she did have some fun while gallivanting around Old Island Marina in the Florida Keys.

Each consecutive kitten seemed to come into the world more easily than the last, and by the time the last two arrived, Brian and I had actually fallen asleep, exhausted from an early morning and a stressful day. Effie would come walk over my face, purring, and run back to the box as if to say *come look, more babies!* When it was over, we counted five: two girls, three boys.

Finnegan, the first born, I named for a good friend who had recently passed away. Finbar was next, named for the Admiral of the Conch Republic Navy. Brian and I decided to name the next one Jacob, as he, for some reason, reminded us both of a classmate from elementary school. We fell asleep before naming the last two, and by morning, one of them had died. I thought it may have been bad luck that we hadn't named him, so now the pressure was on to name the last girl. Brian suggested Mary-Anne, after the mistress of the explorer Cortes for whom the island was named. I liked it. It turned out Brian remembered the story wrong, and her name wasn't Mary-Anne at all, but for the kitten, the name would stick.

Whenever we were dockside, Effie had the proclivity to run off to other boats, especially wooden ones, and for a while the kittens provided the perfect retrieval solution. I would take them from the box she kept them confined to and bring them on deck calling *Effie, I'm stealing your babies!* She would instantly pop out of the hatch of an unoccupied boat, tear down the dock and up my pant leg, grabbing and dragging the kittens by the neck back to the nest she had created.

We stayed a couple of days in Cortes, hitching rides in the pouring rain to explore the tiny island. Whale Harbour was by far my favourite spot for no particular reason, with a population of less than ten, I speculated. The library was the size of my childhood bedroom, with the convenient hours: *Fridays, 1 til 3,* posted on the front door.

A time-consuming and somewhat challenging aspect that defined much of the trip along Vancouver Island was the necessity to time the tides and currents. There were many small passes which had to be transited at slack, or near slack, tide. Currents commonly ran at fifteen knots, and in one case, twenty-five knots at its peak. There were probably hundreds of mountainous islands, and dozens of possible routes to choose from. After moving to Von Dop Inlet for a night at the north end of Cortez, we transited Hole in the Wall, which, our tide book promised would be slack water at 2:00 PM. Arriving at 1:40 after a failed fishing attempt in the nearby popular and supposedly foolproof fishing hole, our cruising guide stated our arrival time would be acceptable for passing through the 'rapids' (when the tide was running at full bore, it really was like river rapids). We expected it to be straight forward, knowing that hundreds of less-experienced cruisers passed through these areas on a regular basis. How bad could it be?

The whirlpools were a couple of feet deep, and the surface bubbled and sprayed over much of our path that lay ahead, giving the impression that rocks were scattered everywhere just beneath the surface. We were being rushed downstream at over ten knots, and going sideways. I kept my eyes on the chart, trying to judge our position by the little coves and points of land I was seeing. There were rocks mid channel, according to the chart, but they were fully veiled by the rapids, and looked like much of the rest of the water in the immediate area: white and frothy. Brian steered for shore to avoid the rocks, but we were still going faster on a perpendicular course. A well-powered fishing boat stopped in a calm offshoot of the channel, seeming a bit concerned and wanting to make sure we made it through to the other side alright, which we eventually did approximately fifteen hellish minutes later. About forty-five minutes after that, a number of sailboats were motoring towards the same pass from the other direction. If it was *that* bad just twenty minutes *before* the slack, just think of what they were going to face more than sixty minutes *after* slack tide. Silly chumps.

We found a wonderful secluded anchorage at a low island surrounded by mountains and seals and jumping fish, protected from the southeast gales that were forecast to arrive sometime after midnight. The current pulled us quickly, again, ninety degrees from where we wanted to go, until we were between the two islands marking the entrance. From there, we had to steer around long strands of kelp that were grazing the surface (the thick seaweed can cause problems if it gets caught in the propeller), but were still attached to the rocks thirty-five feet below. We were joined by a local fishing trawler who came to anchor for the night too. It felt like the calm before the storm. The water was like glass except for the occasional light rain passing, along with some less frightening whirlpools that could be seen outside the entrance of the anchorage.

In morning we awoke to much of the same, aside from the trawler being long gone. There was not a breath of wind, so we motored for the first hour. When the wind came, it came strong, and we were suddenly flying along at eight, nine, then ten knots. A while later the GPS showed we were sailing along at *fifteen* knots, all this in the northern end of the Johnstone Strait, where apparently there is always one to three knots of current *against* a northbound vessel. When sailing in heavy winds, I find there comes a point, even when things are going smoothly, where I feel something is about to give. With only one reef in the mainsail, and no other options for flying any sort of smaller sail, I felt we were overpowered. I think Brian felt the same, so when we were approaching shore and it was time to change course, we didn't feel it was safe to do with the sail raised (a quick or unexpected jibe in high winds can do a lot of damage. I'd ripped reef-points and clews clean off the sails on *Annie Laurie,* and on some boats it can bring down the mast). I was estimating the gusts at forty knots, so we dropped the sail, brought Nirmala to her new course, and looked at the GPS. We were still able to steer and were moving in the direction we wanted to go at seven knots, without a single sail raised.

We drifted along like that for a couple of hours, and noticed that the water temperature in the past twenty miles had dropped from sixteen degrees Celsius to eight degrees. This temperature change brought a change in wildlife too. Dolphins played on the bow, and later that afternoon, Brian spotted our first orcas of the trip. There were five of them, and the two largest had dorsal fins that looked taller than Brian, which was an awesome sight as they came within a few meters of the boat.

The wind was relentless until we arrived in Port McNeill that night. I made a phone call to my friend Chris, whom I hadn't seen in a couple of years, who just happened to be cruising the same waters at the time. We'd come within a few miles of each other a couple of times, not knowing until after the fact. An experienced sailor and an officer in the Canadian Coast Guard, when I finally got a hold of him, I told him of our experience at Hole in the Wall.

"Of course, Laura, you add an hour to all the tides this time of year, right?"

The tide tables published by the Canadian Hydrographic Service didn't factor daylight saving time into their tide predictions. That explained the violent eddies and whirlpools and powerful currents, and that parade of boats heading for Hole in the Wall an hour and a half late. I love those learning experiences where, for some reason, nature is kinder than she has to be, and lets chumps like us off with just a warning.

We waited on the weather for a couple of days at Port McNeill, thirty-five to forty-five knots from the southeast that never seemed to come. We took the opportunity to take what must be the smallest BC Ferry in operation over to Alert Bay, on Cormorant Island. The tallest (at one time, anyway) totem pole in the world sits at the top of the hill above the town. Another area of totem poles lay as private memorials of the Namgis tribe down on Pine Street, which runs along the waters edge. As tourists, we were only permitted to view them from the road. Some appeared centuries old, others as if the last touches of paint had been applied just yesterday. Walking back from the tallest totem, we were stopped by a local who asked us how we were enjoying our visit to their island, and he shared some of his smoked salmon (*Indian candy*, as he called it) that he'd just picked up from his smokehouse.

It would be our last sight of civilization for a while.

Fifteen

Myles Inlet was our first stop after leaving Port McNeill, and we lost one of our little feline crewmembers, Finbar, along the way. It was unexpected; it had been a week since their birth, and though Finbar and Finnegan were considerably smaller than the other two, I thought they were doing all right. We were hours from our next port, and Effie was mourning. I'd heard stories of what cats sometimes do with their deceased young, so I decided it was best not to wait for a land burial, so we buried him at sea. Our thoughts immediately turned to Finnegan, the other runt of the litter. We tried to feed her warmed egg and milk, but she refused. The next morning, she was gone too. A Schooner-brand matchbox was slightly bigger than her tiny body, and we buried her in Myles Inlet by the tidal falls. Effie was lost for a while, searching the boat for her lost kittens, but she eventually let go. She became very protective of Jacob and Mary-Anne, and wouldn't let them get very far from their box before taking them by the scruffs of their necks and dragging them back to their nest.

The next jump north was wide open to the Pacific swells. With a name like Cape Caution, the passage seemed a bit more intimidating than it was in reality. We had good wind, and despite dozens of floating logs scattered around, they were easy to spot and avoid, thanks to the seagulls that used them as a rest stop. Once north of the Cape, we were back in the protection of the Inside Passage. An overnight stop at Pruth Bay was recommended by Charlie, the author of our 1986 cruisers guide we picked up at a sailors exchange a month earlier (it was as good as the day it was written, nothing had changed). Charlie's Charts, as far as we were concerned, had been essential for this trip. During a visit to Vancouver in preparation for our journey, Brian had also purchased American published 'charts', which, upon closer inspection, were not as detailed as we had assumed, and were 'not to be used for navigation'. There are reasons why friends don't let friends shop at a particular popular marine retailer. Without Charlie, we would have been completely lost.

In Pruth Bay we spotted wolf tracks on the white sandy beach, a short hike from the anchorage. The island was the site of a sport-fishing lodge, which had recently closed for the season. Caretakers had just arrived by floatplane, as the islands only winter inhabitants, to look after the property for the winter. They spoke of the wolves as if they were family, and shared the history of the decades-old lodge, pointing out an old cabin where John Wayne stayed when he visited the lodge many years before.

Each day as we sailed further north, the scenery steadily changed. We became completely spoiled with humpback whale sightings. If motoring, we would stop to drift silently as they surfaced: a fin, followed by a huge tail that would swoop up before slipping into the water without a trace of a splash. A more impressive show was to see a lone whale somersaulting and slapping the surface with its long fins, sometimes repeatedly for twenty minutes or longer. The sheer power behind the reverberating sound in such a wild environment is difficult to describe.

When wildlife was absent, the wind and seas calm, the only sound was the ringing in our ears. It wasn't unusual for us to go for days at a time without seeing another boat, or plane, or any other sign of civilization. I had no idea before setting out on the trip that there would be such long stretches of desolation. I wondered how many outlaws may have sought the remoteness of this area, and set up a permanent camp in these mountains, where they'd likely never be found.

Bella Bella was the first community we encountered since leaving Port McNeill. As charming as the name sounds, I found the walk around town depressing. The kids were friendly, the teens looked angry, and the shopkeepers were helpful, much like any other small town. But still, I sensed a difference, perhaps the consequence of a community so isolated from the rest of the province. True, B.C. Ferries made a stop there every few days, and there was nothing to stop a float plane from landing just off the shore anytime, but I think I would find it difficult as a young adult trying to find my life's calling in such isolation. We were easy to spot as we wandered around town, not only as sailors, but also as non-natives, and I sometimes found it difficult to read how the locals felt about tourists in their town.

On our way to Klemtu, I recall seeing *Waterfall Point* on the American 'chart', and I slandered the Americans aptitude at chart making once again for being completely wrong. I assumed a place named Waterfall Point would have a waterfall, but one should never assume. It did eventually begin to make some sense in the following hours when we started counting waterfalls by the dozens. This would continue for many days and miles.

In Klemtu, we learned about what the locals call the Spirit Bear. On rare occasion, two recessive genes combine and a Brown bear is born white. There had been sightings in the last week, so we spent much of our time the next few days scanning the shores as we sailed along, hoping to see him. It never happened.

The only fault we found in Charlie's Charts, which we only began to understand in Klemtu, was that most of the native communities were dry towns (an unsettling flashback to Vineyard Haven). Charlie was a sailor, we thought, so he must know that such information might be considered important and would deserve a mention. After two long, dry weeks, I began working on a design for a flag that, when hoisted, any passing ship would unmistakably recognize as the International Distress Signal for Wine and Baguettes, and to assist if possible.

Charlie never steered us wrong when it came to good anchorages though, and he recommended one in Butedale next to an impressive waterfall, as he put it. We entered the small bay, the site of an old cannery, where an old man name Lou was now the caretaker of the remains of the cannery and surrounding buildings. He lived alone, since the 1980's from what I could understand, and advertised on a large piece of plywood by the shore that he sold ice cubes, ice cream, and showers. We tied up to his floating dock, which easily became submerged as we stepped off the boat. He recommended that we do the hike to the nearby lake. Hundreds of felled trees remained behind in the lake, cut decades ago and now gathered in one corner before the top of the waterfall. Since arriving in British Columbia, I'd been dreaming of running around on the log booms and trying my feet at logrolling.

Discovering that lake of huge trees was, unquestionably for me, one of the highlights of the trip. There was yet another degree of silence we experienced up there, as we made our way as close to the middle of the lake that the huge floating logs would allow.

Night was falling, so we began our hike back to Lou's cabin. Lou seemed delighted with the company, and after my lukewarm shower by the light of an LED headlamp strung above the faucet, we all sat around his television to watch a very old Michael Douglas movie on VHS. Lou mumbled a running commentary on the film he'd probably seen hundreds of times, pausing only to top up his glass of vodka and purple Kool-Aid.

Before departing the next morning, Lou told us of a hot spring at the end of an inlet off the beaten track. We sailed up the inlet, dropped the anchor and canoed up the river we assumed Lou had been trying to describe. A short hike into the woods we found the springs. A concrete pool was built around a tiny spout, and the rate of flow was slow, so it wasn't as warm as we'd hoped, but was worth the trip nevertheless.

By evening we were in Hartley Bay, another native town, and very unique in the sense that the entire town was interconnected by boardwalk. There were a couple of scooters, but other than that, the only motorized vehicles on the island were the fishing boats. We followed one walkway up into the woods, where three young boys were walking back from the lake with a big salmon, and very thoughtfully and casually warned, "*Be careful of the bears.*" I still wanted to see a bear, so was eager to keep going, but Brian said he'd better get back to town because it was time to phone his mom, so we turned and headed for home. I know the truth though, Brian.

Some days seemed longer than others, especially when there was little wind, and we were just puttering along with the outboard motor. There's a tendency to fall into a sort of highway hypnosis at the helm, and the boredom can lead to too much thinking. To avoid this, we began to take turns reading to one another to pass the time. I found a book in a second-hand shop in Squamish called *Ralph Edwards of Lonesome Lake*, about a pioneer in the Bella Coola area. Knowing we'd be sailing in the vicinity, I thought it might be of some interest, and it was probably the best dollar I had spent on the entire trip. Ralph's family became caretakers for the wintering Trumpeter swans, which were dwindling in numbers and were dangerously close to extinction. He was credited for getting the species off the endangered list, which was only the beginning of his fascinating story.

Most places we visited we kept to just an overnight stay, either exploring on arrival, or getting up in the morning for a few hours of canoeing or fishing before moving on to our next destination. I would have enjoyed another day or two in Hartley Bay, but we pushed onward, up Grenville Channel to an anchorage in West Inlet. It was deserted aside from a large converted freighter on a mooring called the Heli-Forester. It was a portable accommodation for a logging company that does all of its logging using helicopters. We dropped the anchor in about thirty-five feet of water, and decided we'd like to canoe over to the Heli-Forester and see who was around.

Only one caretaker was aboard, waiting for the next crew to arrive in a few days. We talked for an hour or two, and he described the process by which helicopters plucked the felled trees from the hillside and dropped them into the water, where they'd later be transferred to barges and shipped away. We had a good yarn and it was pitch dark by the time we paddled the canoe back to the boat. As we approached *Nirmala*, I was busy looking below the canoe, splashing the water with my paddle to activate the phosphorescence. Once near the boat, I thought I could see leaves suspended about three feet below the surface, as if on an interface between two layers of water. It turned out to be a water-*mud* interface, more commonly known as the bottom.

"Brian, I think the boat is aground..."

I felt terrible, thinking about how it was *I* who had dropped the anchor, so as I let out the chain, I should have been able to estimate more accurately the depth of the water. The tidal range was substantial, but not quite thirty-five feet. Brian became very quiet for a while as he assessed the situation, and, not being able to read his facial expressions in this darkness, I got a bit nervous. I felt responsible, and knew how I'd feel if I came back to find *Annie Laurie* sitting on the bottom. I didn't know what to say, and then he spared me with his laughter, "Laura, to tell the truth, I can't believe we made it this far!"

We climbed aboard at the bow, careful to keep her balanced on the keel, and made our way below. By morning we were floating again, and at 6:30 AM the tide was falling rapidly, so we got an early start and enjoyed a good laugh at our own expense, after we were sure there was no harm done. I explained my feelings of guilt about it all, but Brian has always been an easy-going and understanding guy. He reminded me how I shouldn't worry my 'pretty little head' about such things, how I couldn't be expected to do a man's work, and why I really was out of my element. A woman's place was in the galley, cooking for her Captain! After watching Brian cook blueberry waffles on the barbecue, and use our only cotton washcloth to clean an inch of solidified bacon fat out of the frying pan, I was more than happy to take on the galley duties.

West Inlet was our final stop before the bustling town of Prince Rupert and the first pub since Vancouver Island. We would regroup here for a couple of days, find a shower for the second time since Port

McNeill, stock up on groceries, do a bit of laundry, and lower the Wine and Baguette distress flag for the first time in three weeks.

Next stop: Alaska.

Sixteen

The day we were to arrive in Alaska began as any other; up before sunrise, a bit of mist in the air, and not much wind. We motored out of Prince Rupert, and within half an hour, the wind picked up. The wind was against us, but we decided to do what we could with it, rather than leave the sails down and motor a more direct course. It would be the first day that we would really have to work for our miles. Days like these were character building, as we wove a zigzag course up Dixon Entrance, seemingly making little to no headway after each tack. As the day wore on, we were looking for back-up plans, because we didn't think we would make our destination of Foggy Bay, Alaska before nightfall. It was surprisingly difficult to find a place to anchor for the night. For an anchorage to be practical, the water couldn't be too deep, which was the main problem on the west coast. Much of the coastline of British Columbia drops to depths of six hundred feet or

171

more within a few feet of shore. Coming up with no alternatives, we resigned ourselves to a night-time arrival in Foggy Bay, with only a hand-sketch in Charlie's Charts to follow.

The moon was on the rise as we approached the entrance to the bay, but it wasn't enough to illuminate the rocks that sat just a few feet above the surface on either side, as the diagram showed. From the bow, away from the sound of the engine, I could hear swells breaking on the reef that offered protection from rolling seas once inside the anchorage, but was nothing short of hazardous when trying to get through it. There was enough salt spray in the air that the beam from the spotlight fell flat within a few feet, so was of no use. We tried to think of other options that would give us a better idea of our actual location. We had a brand new hand-held GPS, which would tell us our location within ten feet, but without a map or chart of some sort to plot that latitude and longitude, the numbers didn't mean much.

Then we remembered something. NOAA, the National Oceanic Atmospheric Administration in the United States provided all the charts for U.S. waters free of charge online, and Brian had downloaded some of the charts he thought we may need the previous week. Luckily, there was just enough power left in his laptop to bring up the necessary chart. We plotted our position on the screen, and then were able to plot a compass course to follow, and we winded our way past a few more shallow spots and islands and dry reefs before finally dropping the anchor at 10:30 PM. It can be frustratingly confusing navigating in the dark. Just when you think you know exactly where you are, and identify the silhouettes of the islands and rocks and think you know what's what when making comparisons to the sketches in the guidebooks, you begin to proceed between the two islands only to realize there is just one. Nights like these, we went slowly. It was interesting to see all the obstacles we had dodged as we departed in daylight the following morning.

The following day was our first official day in Alaska. Ketchikan is the first Port of Entry where you can clear customs when arriving from the south. Effie made sure she would be the first among us to set foot on Alaskan ground, and she took a flying leap off the boat when we were still a fair distance from the dock. Like I mentioned earlier though, since the arrival of the kittens we never had to worry about her going too far.

Ketchikan is a small town that caters largely to cruise ships. We awoke the following morning to no less than six cruise liners clogging the entire waterfront. The town was on the island of Revillagigedo, which eventually became Re-Village Gigolo to Brian and I as we struggled to grasp the proper pronunciation. We stayed long enough for Brian to celebrate his birthday in style, if by accident, when we ended up at a local pub and in the company of a lumberjack who had quite literally just stumbled out of the woods. He called himself Red, had a three-foot beard, and wore a red bandana and red-and-black plaid flannel shirt. He spent the evening ringing the brass bell at the end of the bar, which meant he was buying yet another round of drinks for the house. He passed out money for the jukebox and told us to pick *songs from the soul* and bragged how he lived *totally off the grid, man,* which, in his books, meant kerosene lamps and candles.

Brian and I came to the realization around the same time as one another that it was time to start thinking about heading home. We had reached our destination, and having set out late in the sailing season, the weather was deteriorating rapidly. Not only was the temperature becoming unbearably cold at night, but also the Pacific storms were rolling in, one after another.

We decided to circumnavigate Re-Village Gigolo, which would take a few days and take us through the Misty Fjords National Park. We were a hundred years too late if we wanted to see any sea-level glaciers. A glacier that graced our northernmost anchorage in the early 20th century had receded so far up the valley and around the bend that it would take a full day of hiking to reach its edge.

We were blessed with three days of sunny

weather and decent winds for the circumnavigation. The National Parks people provided moorings to tie off to, so finding a place to anchor wasn't an issue. After tying to a mooring in Punchbowl Cove, we decided to hike up to Punchbowl Lake, on the recommendation of the Visitors Center employee in Ketchikan. Upon canoeing ashore, Brian spotted some fresh bear poop and prints. As eager as I was to see a bear, I was uneasy with the prospects of coming face to face with one in such a remote area. We spent half an hour tiptoeing around, looking for more evidence, or any rustling in the trees. We made our way toward the waterfall, figuring we'd find a trail up to the lake. As we quietly stepped along the rocky shore, we suddenly heard a deep roar. Stopping in our tracks, we looked at one another, and carefully started taking steps backwards, only to realize a moment later it was only a jet, high above our heads.

The lake was lifeless and silent. As a previous visitor had noted in the guest book at the shelter, God forgot to put fish in the lake. The shelter was supplied with an axe and wood for chopping, a fire-pit, raised wooden platforms for sleeping and paddles for an upturned canoe by the waters edge. Though the water was shockingly cold, it was fresh, so I took advantage of it with my soap and shampoo, knowing it might be some time before I'd find a shower again.

Wanting to get to another anchorage twenty

miles south before dark, we limited ourselves to an hour at the lake before hiking back to our canoe and leaving the mooring by early afternoon.

There is a very distinct rock formation mid-channel a few miles out of Punchbowl Cove known as New Eddystone. It's the remnants of the core of a volcano, much like the outcrops on which Edinburgh and Stirling Castle in Scotland are built, the hard rock core remaining where the softer surroundings have eroded away. Captain Vancouver, who was assigned by Britain to survey the coast from California to Alaska late in the 18th century, reportedly stopped and had lunch on the rock. We passed within a half-mile of the rock without seeing more than a slightly smudged dark patch in the fog bank. If Vancouver was surveying these waters in typical west coast weather, it's more likely that he ran his ship *into* the rock, rather than had lunch *on* it.

We crept along, following the barely visible shoreline all the way to our next anchorage, the fog being so thick at times that if we had been mid channel, we would have been unable to see either shore. We picked up a mooring at the mouth of a river where dead salmon were abundant ('tis the season), and a bald eagle watched patiently atop a dead cedar, searching for a suitable dinner. Brian caught our dinner this particular evening, the first (and only) fish of any substance of our trip, a flounder. As juveniles, their eyes are on opposite sides of their head, and they swim upright, like a salmon. At some point, one eye migrates to the same side as the other, and the fish begins to swim like a flatfish along the seafloor, with both eyes on top. Ours was halfway through the metamorphosis, looking like a sad cartoon character that had just had an Acme anvil dropped on his head. Supper that night was delicious.

Before heading back to Canada, it was necessary to re-stock in Ketchikan. The wind was dead calm and the fog left us with less than twenty feet of visibility. It can be bad enough navigating in the fog when you have radar and charts, but we had neither. We were entering a narrow and busy channel with significant currents, frequented this time of year by as many as half a dozen cruise ships per day, along with any number of tour boats and tugs and barges. We estimated our position then set a compass course and noted the time, and calculated when Pennock Island would appear from the fog. Quite some time passed and there was no sign of land. I was on the bow, looking for shallow areas, still unable to see more than twenty feet ahead.

The fog was playing tricks with my vision. I would think I could see land, and then the shape would evaporate. Eventually we found land, but as we followed along, we realized we were at least two miles from where we had hoped. We began bumping (not *quite* literally) our way up the channel, overshooting

177

our desired points over and over, once arriving at a rock pile marked at its low peak by a small green light-house. It was very difficult to do anything else but motor along slowly, and look at the compass, and hope to recognize bits of shoreline that we'd seen a week earlier when we'd entered Ketchikan the first time. A pilot boat, sent ahead of a cruise ship, spotted us on radar and called us on the radio to inform us of the three-hundred-foot ship to follow. The cruise ship eventually called us too, spotting us on their radar. We were unable to see him until, miraculously, the fog lifted long enough to see we were well clear of each other, then closed in once again. Ketchikan was a high-traffic area for float planes as well, and we could hear them overhead, but never did see the ones coming in for a landing this particular day. Floatplane pilot was an occupation that really stirred my interest during my time out west, but in those conditions, I felt much safer in a boat. Even Brian's boat.

In the hopes of quelling any boredom of retracing our steps down the coast, we had hopes of cruising a portion of Haida Gwaii, previously known as the Queen Charlotte Islands. We made the jump across Hecate Straight to Charlotte City, but after a week of waiting out forty-knot winds, we decided to take the short weather window to get back to the mainland, before being inundated with another week of gale force winds. Not many cruisers make it to the west coast of

Haida Gwaii, so we were determined for a while to be one of the lucky few, but it just wasn't to be.

A second stop in Prince Rupert and an interaction with a gentleman named Jean-Marc set us on a different course, one in search of the coastal wolves. He lived aboard the aluminum sailboat he'd built, and had plenty of stories to share. Brian recognized his boat as being from a documentary about the coastal wolves. Jean-Marc told us where our best bet was to see the wolves for ourselves, the north end of Banks Island.

Banks Island was a pleasant day sail away. Anchoring a mile off shore, we launched the canoe at sunset, which coincided with the low tide, when the wolves were likely to wander down to the beach to feast on the exposed shellfish. We quietly sat in the canoe, just off the beach, until we were so cold we were slurring our speech. Once back aboard *Nirmala,* we could hear distant howls. A morning walk on the beach revealed a few sets of prints, but again, this experience was not meant to be.

One day blended into the next as we turned our efforts to getting back to Squamish as quickly as possible. The travel kitty was running low, and the weather was showing no signs of improving before next spring. One week after our search for the coastal wolves in the desolation of the Inside Passage, we were home in Squamish.

§§§

"Two Grande extra-hot half-sweet non-fat no-whip extra foam hazelnut decaf lattes."

If money grew on trees, I would have reserved a flight back to Florida as soon as *Nirmala's* lines were tied to the Squamish dock. Instead, I now stood behind the coffee machine making various espressos at Starbucks, finding it hard to believe that a year ago today, I was two hundred miles offshore in the North Atlantic, sitting in the cockpit of *Annie Laurie.* The atmosphere looked like winter and smelled of salt, and we were bundled up and in high spirits in anticipation of our final destination, Cuba. It's hard not to speculate, could I have known back then what the future had in store, if I ever would have even begun such a journey. Weighing the good with the bad over the past twelve months though I knew it was a decision I would never regret. Certain details I would like to delete from my life story, but I suspect had I stayed home and continued my forecasting position, my life would have spiralled into an unsettled tangle of unrealized dreams and discontent.

As much as we worry about the future and how we're going to live it, there's no telling where all the little choices we make in the run of a day will eventually lead us. Any plans we make have little purpose other than putting our minds at ease for the time being; chances are they'll bear little resemblance to where we find ourselves six months or a year down the line. What got me through those land-bound days were the hopes of earning the means to head back to *Annie Laurie* in early spring, dreams of a jaunt to the Bahamas, and a summer cruise up the eastern seaboard, hopefully arriving in Lunenburg in time for the September Classic boat race. As life unfolded, some of those dreams came true.

Making the most of what you have while working for what you want is a motto I strive to live by. I constantly remind myself how life can pass you by while you're busy making other plans. I tried my best to make the most of my time in British Columbia, enjoying the company of the new friends I had made, while working to enable the next part of my voyage.

It was a challenge though, this business of sitting still. I'd always found clarity in motion, though I felt only loosely responsible for all the adventures that had come my way thus far. I felt I'd been drifting along a dark river, carried by the currents as I tread water. I rarely tried to argue with fate, and I never felt the latitude of my existence had been hindered. Despite having the comfort of past experience telling me everything always finds a way of working itself out, during that winter in Squamish, I couldn't always be convinced that events were unfolding the way they should. Without being able to identify what I seemed to be missing or waiting for, I saw no better option or need to do anything *but* allow that current to take me where it would.

And looking back on it now, I'm glad I didn't make a break for the riverbank.

Seventeen

There she sat, quietly, proudly, and aside from a few fish carcasses left over from an osprey who had taken up residence on her mainmast, *Annie Laurie* was more or less just as I had left her six months earlier.

Leaving British Columbia was, in the end, bittersweet. I said goodbye to wonderful roommates, Kellie and Dan, who became Mary-Anne's adoptive parents, and to my friend Marie, Jacob's new mom. My very brief stint with the Squamish Pipe Band added another dimension to my attempted construction of a real life, and I would miss the sociability of the Sunday night practices with everyone. Last but by no means least, I would miss Starbucks, especially the rare moments of quiet, early on Sunday mornings, when my friend Ross and I would just relax and chat about everything under the sun, and I would easily forget that I was at work, and was in fact talking with the store manager.

It was exactly what I tried *not* to do. Find a place I liked, people I loved, and begin establishing a regular way of life. There always came the time to pull the plug, and it only made it harder to move on. All of this compounded with the mistake of going downhill skiing for the first time on a real West Coast mountain a week before my flight. Like I needed yet another reason not to leave.

So here I was, back in Florida, preparing for the most extensive solo journey of my sailing career. My apprehension about sailing to new and shallow waters alone was substantially alleviated by all the help I received from my boat-sitters, Bill and Shirley, as well as Don and his family aboard *Road to the Isles,* who were just down the road. I spent most of my evenings aboard *Road to the Isles*, as well as the colder nights. We had a few overnight lows that surpassed the lows for the week in Squamish, and left the deck slippery with frost. The bitter breeze flowed freely down below, and I awoke with the cold sun earlier than I could bring myself to appreciate. If it wasn't for Effie being a threat to Jib's territory (*Road to the Isles'* resident cat), we would have probably spent all our nights in their warm spare cabin.

I had not particularly been looking forward to certain aspects of my upcoming voyage, especially the thoughts of being alone for extended periods of time. In anticipation of this, I decided to invest in a subscription to Sirius Satellite Radio to keep me company. Having the option of CBC while in the bizarre world of Fox 'news', not to mention an extensive choice of music, it was well worth the thirteen dollars a month.

I had completed running all my halyards and sheets, and the sails were back where they belonged. I replaced my batteries, both for starting the engine as well as supplying electricity for lights and radios, replaced the oxidized and crumbling anchor chain with new, and had completed a thorough scrub-down of the mould factory the boat had become after sitting dormant for six months.

With just a few odds and ends to contend with, I was ready to head down the ICW the following morning. I planned to reconvene with *Road to the Isles* at West Palm Beach later in the week, where we'd wait together for a favourable weather window to cross the Gulf Stream and the final sixty miles to the Bahamas.

§§§

I often reminisce about the beginning stages of the purchase of *Annie Laurie*. Some shared my excitement, others expressed concern, and others dismissed it as little more than a pipe dream. My brother Christopher is generally outspoken with his opinions of the lifestyles of his siblings, and my situation wasn't to be an exception. I remember his words *exactly:* "Laura, you can't just buy a boat and sail off into the sunset. That's something people do when they're old and retired."

He may have been right, in a way. Perhaps with a lifetime of experience behind me, and accumulated friendships and memories, and likely a partner in life, maybe everywhere I went and everything I did would have held more meaning. It was mildly depressing when I found myself nudging Effie to point out a giant sea turtle swimming under the boat, or another breathtaking sunset over the water. She just didn't have the same appreciation for those things.

Not far into this part of the trip, Effie had managed to use up eight of her nine lives. One night, anchored just south of Cape Canaveral, I noticed she had been unusually quiet. I didn't think much of it, and didn't put any serious effort into finding her for a couple of hours. I was having a good time, cooking dinner, and dancing to the reggae music station on Sirius. When I eventually went on deck to see if she'd taken up her usual station in one of the sails, I heard a pathetic, weakened meow. She was under the bowsprit, carefully balanced on the wire stays beneath it, mere inches above the water. Her eyes were as big as saucers as she looked at me awaiting rescue, not daring to move an inch, lest she fall in the water.

And the other seven lives, you might ask? They

vanished instantly a few mornings later, when I awoke to find that she had *chewed through my Sirius satellite radio antenna!* I figured it was retribution for the night of enjoyment I had at Cape Canaveral while she was stranded helpless. But that was no excuse. Later as I was fetching buckets of salt water to wash the deck, she was foolish enough to come and stand at my feet. I never would have thought something so cruel could make me feel that much better, but it did. Go ahead Mom, call the SPCA.

With some careful tampering, and patience I never thought I would find, the antenna was receiving a signal once again. I was eventually able to forgive Effie, but for some time later, my first words to her each morning were, "Good morning, mommy's girl. Remind me, how many lives do you have left?"

As planned, I met up with *Road to the Isles* at West Palm Beach, where we only had to wait for two days for our weather window to cross the Gulf Stream. The morning of departure, I was out of my bunk by 2:30 AM, up the mast with my headlamp on, doing some last-minute fixes with my problematic roller-furling sail. I put the kettle on for coffee, and listened to the latest weather forecast and the current conditions elsewhere along the Florida coast. Shortly after 4:00 AM, still half asleep, I set the mainsail, hauled up the anchor and made my way out the Lake Worth inlet. It was generally calm, about two to three foot waves just outside the inlet, aside from one square breaking wave (as a result of opposing wind and tide), which put the bow underwater, a spoke from the helm into my ribs, and sent everything that wasn't properly stowed airborne. *Now* I was awake.

During my evenings on the waterway, after dinner and settling into my bunk, I wrote five letters and placed them in empty wine bottles, which I tossed overboard every few miles as I crossed the Gulf Stream. Having heard so many intriguing stories of the circumstances of seagoing messages, I was hoping my action would create an intriguing story of my own someday, when and if any of the bottles were ever found.

Fourteen hours and roughly seventy-five miles later, I crossed the divide between dark blue mile-deep water and the beautiful turquoise sea beyond the reef. I eventually caught up with *Road to the Isles*, who left hours after I did, but managed to overtake me along the way. We anchored in twenty feet of water on the crystal clear Bahama Banks at dusk, not a breath of wind, and no land in sight.

I was surprised at how quickly I adjusted to shallow water. I was dreading it, thinking I'd have a heart attack over any approaching dark spot ahead, expecting it to be a coral head, and for an unavoidable one to clip the side of my hull and split it open. Instead, as I set a course for Green Turtle Cay (pronounced *key)* to clear Customs, I found myself taking pleasure in observing the slimy cylindrical creatures on the bottom, the *giant* turtles, dolphins that seemed overjoyed at *Annie Laurie*'s presence, and the shadow of my hull and sails over the sandy bottom only seven feet below.

Like the shallows, being alone wasn't so bad either. When I really thought about it, I wasn't alone at all. Meeting people while sailing is often the result of a chain reaction. Mine began while at anchor at Green Turtle Cay, when the wind picked up behind a passing frontal system. Dragging anchor in a crowded anchorage is a great way to meet people. Within minutes, three dinghies converged on my boat and we set my second anchor, which after re-setting a few times, eventually held. That's how I met Dave, Sid, and Jerry. Jerry invited me over for a drink that evening, where I met Jim and Jeff.

The following day, noticing Jeff's anchor was dragging, I rowed over to help, arriving at the same time as Charlie. That evening, Charlie came by to invite me for dinner, where I met his dad, Charlie Sr., and their friends Raffi, Lisa, Brenda, and Webb. Charlie also introduced me to Trevor and Brendon, twenty-year-old Canadians who sailed down from Kingston, Ontario aboard *My Life,* a tiny steel sailboat they had rebuilt themselves with the help of a *Welding for Dummies* book from their local library (I thought *I* was hard-core). *Road to the Isles* introduced me to another couple down from Nova Scotia, Heather and Peter, who introduced me to their friends Jason, Mike, and Sward, all sailing solo. And to my great surprise and delight, who else was at anchor at Green Turtle Cay but my old friends aboard *Pathos*, Mike and Jan, whom I met back in Cape May, New Jersey on my way down the coast sixteen months earlier.

No, I really couldn't say I was alone. When I dropped my anchor, popped the cork from my bottle of champagne, and sat back to listen to the songbirds welcoming the coming of night, I thought of my brother's words once more, and was grateful to have arrived at White Sound, Green Turtle Cay on my 29th birthday, and not my 65th.

§§§

The following week, I met up with a friend of friends from Charleston (their attempt at matchmaking a couple of eligible young sailors, I believe). A solo-sailor on his way back to South Carolina, Banff aboard *Blue Magic* dropped his anchor next to mine outside of Hopetown. An excellent sailor and spear-fisher, we spent a couple of days going out to the reef in his zodiac. Until now, I had been satisfied diving for conch (the stationary targets that they are), but now I was very enthused to try my own hand at spearfishing. With this new skill, I looked forward to the coming months of practice as I planned to sail further south into Eleuthera and the Exumas.

Failing miserably at fishing during those days, I at least managed to dive for one good-sized conch. Banff suggested it would make a great conch horn, so a horn it became. It's a bit of a tradition, among the cruising boats at least, to blow conch horns at sunset. That evening, Banff showed me how it was done. I used to be critical of the boaters who took part in this nightly custom; I always said it was rather cheesy. That remained true, and from then on, I joined them.

Banff made a living working on boats, and was able to deal with many things I'd gradually become completely fed-up with. Problems had compounded to the point where I couldn't choose which one to tackle, so I did nothing. I was simply overwhelmed. My sink was completely clogged, so I couldn't do dishes. Both of my stove burners were on the fritz because I didn't invest in the higher quality kerosene they required, and bread and peanut butter was growing old quickly. And of course there were those things I gave up on a long time ago, the depth sounder and autopilot, neither of which had *ever* worked. Each morning, Banff showed up to tackle another problem, and he wasted no time, obviously in his element. With the galley back in order, he turned to the depth sounder, which was fully installed and transducer embedded in the bilge in no time. A working depth sounder, while obviously not essential (heck, I made it this far), was a very nice thing to have. And, while not having the means to fix the autopilot completely, he at least discovered it was the electric motor that was causing the issues.

Hopetown was a stopover until a weather window opened for his final four hundred nautical mile sail home to Charleston, and after a week of good times, one evening he was headed for the break in the reef to head offshore. I frequently struggle with what should be minor decisions, and I couldn't decide whether I should stay in Hopetown for a while longer to see him off, or just continue my journey southward. I felt torn and indecisive, then as he was making final preparations to get underway, I weighed anchor first and headed south.

That evening I was anchored a few miles south in relatively calm seas and utter blackness off Tillo Cay with a strong southeasterly breeze blowing. Listening to the distant surf break, I was thinking how rough the seas must be on the Atlantic side of the reefs. For Banff's sake, I was willing the moon to come up a little sooner that night, and now understood why I left Hopetown when I did: I never did like the feeling of being the one left behind.

Eighteen

A day or two after leaving Hopetown, I was reunited with Trevor and Brendon aboard *My Life*. They had thoroughly enjoyed a local full moon party near Tillo Cay a few days earlier, and as a result had missed their weather window to cross to Eleuthera. I was glad they did.

We stayed at Tillo for a few days, swimming and spearfishing and observing our first launch of a rocket from Cape Canaveral. Brendon and I snorkelled around a small reef indicated by a cruising guide, Brendon successfully spearing a lobster, which he hurried back to the dinghy. I continued to take aim at various fish, mostly snapper (I could never bring myself to take aim at grouper, after a friend referred to them as the Golden Retrievers of the Sea), but I honestly spent more time diving to the bottom to retrieve my runaway spear. The largest fish to come within range was a three-foot barracuda. They're usually harmless, so long as you're not wearing sparkling jewellery, which they may mistake for prey. They can be mildly intimidating, as they show no fear of the spear being aimed in their direction. In fact, none of the fish I took aim at seemed very concerned, and would just passively watch as the metal spear floated past them, then would congregate to the pole as soon as it came to rest in the sand. Perhaps they were all just experienced prey, and instinctively knew after taking one look at me that I wasn't a serious threat to their well-being.

Later in the day, Brendon speared a large amberjack. I rowed over to the rocky outcrop he had climbed onto (when the blood of a fish starts to flow, the sharks aren't far behind) and delivered the fish back to *My Life*, where Trevor (crew and chef) took on the task of cleaning the fish. We ate well that night; lobster and wine as appetizer, fish and wine for main course, and wine for dessert. I'm not sure what sparked my memory, but I suddenly remembered that the rocket launch from Cape Canaveral had been rescheduled for that evening. We didn't know what time, so we put the VHF on channel 68, where there was constant chatter among cruising boats, and someone announced it was five minutes to launch time. The trajectory was to be over Great Sale Cay in the northern Bahamas, and the sky was clear. I'd like to give a riveting description of it, but I cannot (maybe if I had skipped dessert?). I remember it leaving behind an interesting glowing blue cloud for a few minutes afterward. Trevor hopped on 68 to see if anyone knew what it was. The only answer received was one quiet male voice flatly and definitively declaring it was God.

We were fortunate to pick up a very strong wireless signal at Tillo Cay (cleverly labeled 'The Coconut Telegraph') and getting a weather forecast was easy. We were all eager to head over to Eleuthera. This would involve one more day sail to take us to the southern Abacos, which would be our launch point to make the fifty-mile crossing over the open Atlantic the following day. We picked our window, and sailed down to Lynyard Cay on St Patrick's Day. A very weak norther was forecast for the day after, fifteen knots from the northeast. It sounded perfect. We'd cross the reef just south of Lynyard Cay at the crack of dawn, have a lovely sail with the wind behind us and ten to twelve foot seas, comfortably and broadly spaced, and cross the reef at Eleuthera before dark.

Fifteen knots? There must be a formula that exists that allows one to calculate what the actual winds will be, based on what the forecast claims they will be. In this case, it was multiply by two and add five. Twenty-five knots all night, and by morning, frequent squalls that brought winds of thirty-five knots and probably higher, torrential rains and nearby chain lightning that sent me running to disconnect my radio antenna and switch the selector switch to my boat batteries to OFF. Needless to say, we didn't weigh anchor once awaking to such conditions. One large gust heeled the boat over about twenty degrees and broke my anchor free of its hold in the part-sand, part-seagrass bottom. *My Life* was suddenly getting bigger. I started grabbing fenders that I had tucked down below and was preparing to throw them between the two hulls to ease the impact of the impending collision, but then I felt the tug of the anchor grabbing hold of the bottom again, and, like a well-rehearsed dance, *My Life* started dragging *her* anchor. When the boats were once again a safe and comfortable distance apart, their anchor dug again, and the excitement was over. We wouldn't be departing for Eleuthera today.

Two days later, we had another weather window and departed. It was a sloppy day of motoring to begin with; no wind, but large swells still remained from the windy days before. By mid-afternoon, we had a gentle east wind and set some sail. As soon as I set my genoa, my engine started making the now-familiar racing sound that meant it was being starved of fuel. In rough seas, the fuel would slosh around the old steel tank, and little bits of rust and crud would clog the fuel filter. Knowing what a pain it had been in the past to bleed the air out of the fuel lines after replacing the filter, I resolved to not deal with it until the boat was anchored. Now all I could do was pray for more wind, so we could cross the reef before sunset. When the wind came in late afternoon, it came strong, and I was under full sail as I crossed the reef north of Little Egg Island. Thankfully I had good, accurate charts on loan from Banff, and I was able to adjust my original plan to cross the reef at a good point of sail, about fifteen minutes before sunset.

I had not followed one of my most important rules that I strove to adhere to, and that was to *never* rely on my engine. Any journey I made, I asked myself, "If I didn't have an engine, would I be able to make this trip under sail alone?" The fact that we were playing chicken with another (and much stronger) approaching norther, and a forecast of little to no wind for the crossing itself, left me wondering why I had taken the risk by deciding to weigh anchor that morning. I didn't have an answer.

I am indebted to *My Life*, who stuck with me the whole way, even when it originally seemed that we all would be crossing the reef after dark. Once through the reef, and unable to sail any closer to the wind to get closer to shore, they threw me a tow line and towed me close to the southern shore of Royal Island, where we hoped we'd have a bit of protection from the upcoming front.

That evening, we decided we'd have conch fritters for supper with the conch we'd been saving. I'd been keeping mine in a mesh bag, and when I wasn't underway, I hung them in the water to keep them alive.

More than once I forgot about them and looked back to see them water-skiing. After two hours of hammering shells and tenderizing the meat, we had our fritters. We concluded, though, it was too much mess and effort, and resolved to not bother picking up any more conch if we came across them.

Had we known what the next three days had in store for us, we probably would have bit the bullet that night and tried to transit the narrow entrance, even under the shroud of complete darkness, into the protected harbour of Royal Island (with *My Life* employed as tugboat) while the winds were still manageable.

The following morning, I turned on my VHF to see what boats were around, and was surprised to hear *Road to the Isles*. They had left the Abacos close to a month earlier Cuba-bound, so I hadn't expected to see them again this season. They had a change of plans, and were seven miles away, sitting at the entrance to Spanish Wells. I couldn't wait to get there and see them again.

By this point, the weather had deteriorated significantly, and I had already completely drained my start battery by trying to start the engine after changing the fuel filter, which stubbornly held onto those pockets of air. *My Life* refused to leave me there alone, despite their boat being substantially smaller, and therefore more susceptible to the uncomfortable motions caused by the rough seas. They brought over a portable generator, in the terrible weather, in a dinghy that barely floated at the best of times, and we tried again to start the engine, to no avail. Don aboard *Road to the Isles* strongly advised that we get into a more protected area before the full brunt of the norther hit, and I wanted nothing more. *My Life* with her outboard was no longer powerful enough to tow *Annie Laurie* in the rough seas, so Brendon offered to come along and help me weigh anchor so we could attempt sailing towards safe harbour. It was worth a try.

The wind was too strong to have the mainsail set, so we had the small jib and mizzen sail at our disposal. I needed the boat to ultimately end up seven miles due east of my current position, but with twenty-five knots of wind coming directly from the east, even as we sailed as close to the wind as we could, the boat was making so much leeway (being blown sideways), we were ultimately going *west*. I looked ahead to see seagrass reaching the surface, and I wasn't entirely confident of our exact location. I knew there were rocky shoals in the area, so I turned the boat around and started heading to where we had been anchored. Once the anchor was down again, *Annie Laurie* was further away from Royal Harbour than when we started. Sailing to safety was not going to be an option.

As the winds continued to build, the boat was hobby horsing violently, burying the bow under the waves on a regular basis. Trevor had motored out with their dinghy with my second anchor as a back-up, but still, the *sound* of the stress and strain on the bow where the anchor line was tied made me feel sick to my stomach. I was just *waiting* for something to crack or break. We tried to distract ourselves by having a few drinks and playing card games. That was quickly halted when I went on deck to find their dinghy being hung vertically on my stern. Their outboard engine was underwater, and only a bit of the bow of the dinghy was still above the surface. Grabbing the dinghy line, we pulled it alongside, and reached for the outboard. Everything seemed in slow motion as the motor slipped off the back of the dinghy and began its descent to the bottom. Trevor immediately praised himself for having tied the engine to the dinghy with a safety line. We had one more chance. Trevor grabbed a big knife from the galley, and with one whack on the taut line, the outboard was free and we pulled it aboard. Now it became a race against time to get *their* engine running before it seized. Oy vey.

Roughly two hours passed. We put the outboard in a bucket of water and took turns cranking it. Brendon pulled out the spark plugs to rinse, dry and clean them, then we continued cranking, and the cursing and swearing that ensued as they periodically sustained minor shocks from holding the engine in the wrong place gave us reason to laugh at our predicament, all the while Trevor never lost a hold of his beer, as we wondered what the hell could possibly happen next. It was probably around that time that I noticed my bilge pump coming on a little more often than usual.

They eventually saved their outboard, and my pump kept up with the increase in water that was entering the bilge. Another rough, sleepless night ensued, and the next morning *My Life* had to weigh anchor and head into Spanish Wells to find their friend who was flying in from Canada. Unable to bear the thoughts of a third night out in such conditions, especially alone, I made another effort to find the trouble-shooting manual for my Perkins diesel. After tearing every leaf of paper from bookshelves, drawers, cupboards and cubbies, I finally found the book. It was only a matter of bleeding two valves I had missed on my fuel pump, and within an hour, the engine was running like a champ. I somehow managed to haul up both thirty-pound anchors and accompanying chain simultaneously (lifting car off trapped child scenario), and I called *Road to the Isles* to say I was on my way to Spanish Wells. Three hours later I dropped my anchor beside them, in much calmer waters.

I'm still not sure why exactly *Annie Laurie* began to take on so much water during those few days. As is typical of boats, the actual source of the leak is often in a space too small to crawl into, so while I could see the water pouring down the inside of the hull, the precise origin of the leak remained a mystery. With more strong southerly winds in the forecast, we backtracked to Royal Island, a virtual hurricane hole. There, I spent time in the water attempting to caulk the area around the shaft that holds the rudder in place. I couldn't think of any other explanation of how the water was getting in. After an hour in the water, the leak didn't appear to slow at all. Frustrated, I gave up.

Over the next day or two, I thought long and hard about packing it in. It wasn't just the leak; there were a multitude of troubles that had been systematically arising, all seeming to indicate that a decision to begin heading north now would be wise. I had become overwhelmed with the amount of maintenance on the boat that I had not yet found the time to attend to, and my kerosene cook-stove was preparing to throw in the towel for good. With most things aboard either canned or dried, and the fresh produce available being extortionately priced, I knew my days would be numbered once the stove drew its final breath.

After much pep-talking to myself though, I decided I would soldier on. The bilge-pump was maintaining the leak, the stove wasn't completely useless just yet, and I had no one to blame but myself on the maintenance issue. All of it still needed to be tackled, no matter where I went.

Eventually, *My Life* and I sailed down to Hatchett Bay, which became known to us as Hotel Hatchett Bay (you can check-out any time you like, but you can never leave). The relentless high winds kept us in lock-down in this small anchorage for over two weeks. It used to be a salt-water pond, being fed by blue holes (underwater caves) that lead out to the Atlantic Ocean. A few sticks of dynamite later, the pond became a bay, accessible by a new opening on its western side. The holding (ability of an anchor to grab the bottom) was poor throughout the bay, so the local government, in an attempt to attract more boaters, had placed an array of free moorings to make things easier. With another front in the forecast, and trusting the moorings were strong, we decided to abandon the discomfort of small boats in storms and go ashore to explore.

I had read about the Hatchett Bay Caves in an old *Lonely Planet* guidebook. The directions in the guide were vague, and as we asked around town, the first few locals had no idea what we were talking about. Even if they had never visited the site, you'd expect that they would have at least heard of its existence on this tiny island. It runs half a mile underground, is inhabited by a colony of leaf-nosed bats, and displays charcoal signatures from as far back as the early 1800's, and perhaps earlier. The earliest date I saw was 1832, and to put that in my own personal context, those names were scrawled the same year my ancestors set out from Greenock, Scotland, on a ship bound for Canada.

There was little more than an old weathered sign propped up against a small stone wall off the main road. If you weren't looking for it, you'd probably miss it. I thought if a similar cave were in Canada or the States, there would have been a woman collecting an admission fee at the opening, and we'd be broken into groups of eight and led through by a guide, and a proper concrete surface would have paved the bottom for concern of safety (read: lawsuits) and all of our possible graffiti implements would have been confiscated. As it was, we tripped our way over limestone ledges and fallen stalactites and avoided leg-breaking holes with our one dim headlamp, and I was able to use burned sticks from the field around the cave to leave my mark, *Laura and Effie, Annie Laurie, 2009.*

After a hair-raising 100 mile-per-hour hitched ride in the back of a truck to Hatchett Bay, we were thankful to return to our respective boats, and not to have met our sorry end on an Eleutheran road. We stayed in Hatchett Bay for another week, the small opening to escape the bay not looking very inviting to any of us, with constant breaking waves converging and compressing into a space no more than fifty feet across.

One of those days, I took an afternoon and

hitched a ride to a saltwater pond with Beth and Tom from another neighbouring boat, *Fabled Past.* Beth had noticed rock crabs a day earlier and this time came prepared with a net and a cooler. Between the two of them, they rounded up ten sizable crabs from knee-deep water. I tried spearfishing, swimming out a ways into the foggy water, but lost my nerve quickly. A local told Beth that Jacques Cousteau once explored the pond, and after descending into one of the blue holes within it, was horrified by some strange unidentifiable creature he witnessed there. He was unnerved to the point of being unable (or unwilling) to ever talk in detail about what he experienced that day. I'd like to do some research on that claim, but the story was sufficient to keep me from doing any extensive exploration of my own that day.

Once liberated from Hotel Hatchett Bay, we all sailed twenty miles south to Governors Harbour. It seemed to be geared more towards tourists than our other stops in Eleuthera. The town was tiny and attractive, well kept and well provisioned (*four* liquor stores). I hit up the local bakery for some specialty coconut and cinnamon bread, and the grocery store had the sweetest tomatoes I've had since the ones from the vine of Mom's tomato plant at the cottage. The town had decent water from many available taps along the road, which was a rarity in Eleuthera. Most available water was salty water: seawater subjected to reverse-osmosis, but with poor results. Though many locals were brought up on it, my stomach wouldn't accept it. It was well worth hanging around Governors Harbour a few extra hours to ferry jugs back and forth to top up my water tank while the opportunity was there. Leaning over to the tap suspended from a wall of tiles, the upward draft was blowing my skirt skyward, Marilyn Monroe-style. It was a quiet morning, and not seeing anyone around, I made little effort to do anything about it; I was busy, one hand on the tap, and the other holding the jug. When the jug was full, I turned to make my way to the beach, only to see a roly-poly teenager leaning against a tree, holding up his camera-phone, displaying a wide smile as he nodded his head approvingly. I think I made his day.

Another couple of weeks put *My Life, Fabled Past,* and *Annie Laurie* in Rock Sound, near the southern end of Eleuthera. The liquor store was perfectly placed for grabbing a beer for the walk to the grocery store, which they encouraged and gladly opened for you at the counter, and placed it in a small brown paper bag. Anywhere else, we may have looked like alcoholics, but not in the Bahamas. In Rock Sound, we would have felt conspicuous walking around with our hands empty.

One of Rock Sound's attractions was Ocean Hole Park, a landlocked blue hole. A large round crater with shear cliffs for diving, its depth rose and fell with the tide. Fish flipped and snapped at breadcrumbs we tossed on the surface, as Bahamian laughing-gulls tried their best to intercept the tosses.

It was now early May, and the time had come for *Fabled Past* to head north, and *My Life* and *Annie Laurie* to continue south. The Exumas were calling.

Nineteen

Departing Eleuthera early morning, we were anchored north of Highbourne Cay in the Exumas by sunset. En route, *My Life* caught a huge dolphin (the fish, not the mammal), about which they repeatedly broadcast their excitement over on the VHF. That night, we enjoyed the fresh sushi we'd long been waiting for.

The Exumas really were all they're cracked up to be. Unlike Eleuthera, the cays were sparsely inhabited, and the water was crystal clear (you could see the sharks coming). While anchored and snorkelling west of Highbourne, I watched as a nine-foot bull shark skirted the edge of my underwater visibility, the same type of shark that took the arm (along with the spear and the fish it was holding) of a Venezuelan tourist a hundred miles south in Georgetown two weeks earlier. Without a speared fish and its associated blood trail, these sharks are considered to be of little threat to humans.

Highbourne Cay catered primarily to wealthy yachts and sport-fishing boats, so anything of interest to us wasn't ashore, but instead below the surface. We found an excellent shallow reef for snorkelling. On some charts, it was known as the *Octopus' Garden*. On other charts, it didn't exist; the same area was apparently more than twelve feet deep and nothing but sand. It was a good example of why it's inadvisable to travel after dark. Such misprints are easily read in the daylight by keeping a sharp lookout from behind a good pair of polarized sunglasses.

I had heard much of the lore of Normans Cay, where the drug lord Carlos Lehder ran his operation and subsequently earned a life sentence without parole plus 132 years in a U.S. prison. Stories abound of cruising sailboats during the 1970's and 80's being chased by machinegun-wielding guards when they ventured too close to the island. I went ashore to find villas pocked with bullet holes and went for what would become an epic row around the south of the island, to find the airplane destined to pick up a load of cocaine from Lehder that missed the runway in the 1980's. The plane sat in ten feet of water, and sinks a little lower with every passing year. Just a few years ago, the wreck was still in decent enough shape that you could sit in the cockpit as fish swam around your feet. Most of the fuselage was underwater now, and I was able to snorkel through its coral-encrusted casing.

I met a classy couple and their highly intelligent young son aboard a catamaran while anchored at Normans Cay. They provided me with some much-needed stimulation for positive introspection on where this journey was taking me. Hyde offered his expertise with any problems I had aboard, so I mentioned my autopilot. He spent the better part of the following day disassembling the motor, soldering broken connections, calibrating the compass, and going for test runs. By the end of the day, *Annie Laurie* had an autopilot. Three years, thousands of miles, and always a hand at the helm, I now looked forward to my first overnight trip where I could take catnaps while the autopilot kept the course. This opened up a whole new world of possibilities of just how far I could travel on my own, and what additional destinations now existed for me as a solo sailor.

The next couple of weeks were especially memorable, as I spent much time in the Exumas Land and Sea Park. It's a relatively small area (one hundred eighty square miles) where all fishing is prohibited. Warderick Wells, home of the park headquarters, offered moorings in various locations around the cay, either for a nightly fee, or in exchange for a few hours of volunteer work. I'm not sure why, but Brendon from *My Life* seemed to jump at the chance to mix (by hand

and shovel) and pour concrete, which the three of us did on our first day, creating another slab of the cellar floor of the headquarters. The things we do to our bodies when we feel young and invincible. I still feel the pain.

The following day, the park warden allowed me to accompany him and two members of the Royal Bahamian Defense Force as they patrolled the parks waters, in an attempt to enforce the no-fishing regulations and collect mooring fees. He pointed out all the good snorkel spots and moorings and sights to see, which was a great orientation for the following week when I headed further south with my own boat.

After a day aboard the patrol boat, the park warden introduced me to his friend Phil, who'd just arrived aboard *Retriever*, a small cargo boat based in Miami. Phil was tall, with big brown eyes, freckles, and dark flowing hair. He radiated a confidence I wasn't accustomed to observing in men my own age. I was instantly enamoured, though I tried my best to remain aloof.

The following day, Effie and I were invited to join *Retriever* as they offloaded cargo to various private cays within the park. We delivered everything from Cornish hens to diesel generators to cedar shingles. I spent much of those two days laughing more than I had for a long time, meeting the local caretakers of the islands, and just being in some generally unique situations. While underway between islands, I attempted a casual investigation, hoping to learn more about this Phil character. I thought I was being smooth as I dropped probing questions, such as 'What does your wife do?' and 'How do the kids feel when Dad goes to the Exumas for weeks at a time?' After cleverly determining he was free and single, my heart was filled with hope of all the possibilities the future could hold. I no longer felt I was destined to grow old alone.

That evening, after sharing dinner aboard *Retriever*, we took our conversation outside to the foredeck. Asking him when he'd last seen a shooting star, he sadly admitted that he considered the phenomenon sufficiently uncommon that he'd never looked skyward long enough to see one. How our expectations in life can leave us blind. I told him they're not as rare as he might think, as we lay back on the cargo hatch to take in the night sky. A few moments later, he saw his first shooting star, and I saw the beginning of something wonderful.

§§§

I decided the next day I would continue to venture further south. While something felt so *right* with Phil, I reasoned if we were meant to be, circumstance would bring us together again. In any case, he had an itinerary to adhere to. I had my own, though somewhat vague, agenda too and couldn't begin to spend my time following him around like a lost puppy.

I set my destination to Staniel Cay, home of the Thunderball grotto, where scenes from a James Bond movie were filmed. After close to six hours of motor-sailing, the wind increased to twenty-five knots from directly ahead. I gave up when I realized I was making less than one knot towards my destination. I turned off the engine, swung the boat around and sheeted out the main sail and headed for a nearby anchorage at Bell Island. Here, I met Laurel and Mike, who invited me over for dinner moments after I dropped the anchor.

Laurel had been coming to the Bahamas for years, and had taken Mike on as crew. Mike was much younger and very eager to check out all the snorkelling sites, whereas Laurel seemed to possess the *been there, done that* attitude. So with Laurel's fast dinghy, Mike and I were able to visits spots such as a small cave at Rocky Dundas, where at low tide you could swim into, but at high tide, you would have to dive under the wall to come up into the round cave with two-storey walls and a hole in the top, where beams of sunshine descend to illuminate the unique rock formations. Next stop was a small airplane that crashed while allegedly running drugs and was in fifteen feet of water near O'Briens Cay. It was small, and after a quick look,

Mike and I ascended, simultaneously asking one another, 'That's *it?*' We quickly moved on to a tiny rocky outcrop known as the Sea Aquarium, where hundreds of tame fish quickly congregate on any snorkeler, expecting to be fed. It was a popular spot. Many dinghies came and went as we leisurely took in all the details of the fish, coral, and one extraordinarily large turtle.

It took some time to sink in, that the moment I had turned *Annie Laurie* north the previous day, that that was to be the southernmost point of my journey. As long as I had been heading south, I was avoiding thoughts of the return journey, and the accumulating responsibilities of what life back home was going to bring. As I left the anchorage at Bell Island, I watched Mike and Laurel make the turn south for Georgetown, as I made my turn back to Warderick Wells. I felt I had reached a milestone. No more new ground to cover, just a re-tracing of steps. I found those thoughts severely depressing. I spent two more days at Warderick Wells, thinking too much, and finding it a great effort to be social. How much I've missed out on in life when my own thoughts have overcome my ability to see what joy can still exist at any given moment, especially with so many new (though perhaps only temporary) friends around.

Effie almost cashed in her ninth life during our second stop at Warderick Wells. She came along as a group of us, Phil included, went for a party on a houseboat named *Owl* for the evening. Someone spooked her with a life-size and very realistic toy turtle, after which she disappeared, I presumed, to another corner of the houseboat. At 5:00 AM, it became obvious she had disappeared into the water. She was in the park warden's skiff, tied twenty feet off the stern of the houseboat. How she managed to climb aboard the skiff before being swallowed by a shark or barracuda, I'll never know. I guess to protect the innocent, I should admit now that the turtle-bearing *someone* was actually me.

A few days later I awoke early and got underway by 7:00 AM from Warderick Wells, with an absence of farewells. I had expected to spend more time with Phil, but he was busy with *Retriever,* and would soon be bound for his home in Miami anyway. While aboard the *Owl,* we had tentatively decided to meet up the next evening at the weekly bonfire hosted by the Park. The pangs of rejection are reflected in my ship's log, where I scribbled, *"Phil said he would call, but he didn't. Never saw him again."*

I sailed for Highbourne Cay once again, through hours of thunder and lightning storms. It seemed to be just one storm, settling over the boat early in the day and relentlessly following me all the way to my next anchorage. I couldn't have been less concerned about the lightning strikes, even as one bolt struck the water less than half a mile off my stern. It seemed like child's play after sailing the coastal waters of Florida the previous summer.

At Highbourne, I hoped to get to the general store before it closed for the afternoon. It was a long row from the anchorage, against a strong incoming tide, and I began to doubt I was going to make it in time. A couple from another boat were taking their dog Blue ashore, and offered me a tow. I gladly accepted. In the course of conversation, they asked where I was headed next. I told them the Abacos, though I was recently considering Miami, but didn't have good charts between the Exumas and southern Florida. They said it just so happened they had accidentally purchased an extra set of charts for that passage, including Nassau, Andros, and Bimini, and I was welcome to have them.

I made my final decision at that very moment: I was going to Miami.

Twenty

Before leaving the northern Exumas, there was one more anchorage to explore. Just a stone's throw from Highbourne lay Allan's Cays, an attraction for its resident iguana population. In addition, it was reasonably protected from all wind directions. Going ashore to feed the iguanas would be my last adventure with Brendon and Trevor. The iguanas were aggressive and intimidating and would barrel towards us in an awkward fashion, threatening to chew on our toes, it seemed, if we weren't careful. I had watched high-speed tour boats from Nassau take people ashore throughout the day before I ventured in, and I was quietly scoffing at all the girls in bikinis who would squeal whenever the prehistoric creatures approached. I was embarrassed when I learned that it *too* was my natural reaction, to scream like a girl, when one came running towards me, claws out and staring intently.

I made the executive decision to change my fuel

filter while anchored in Allan's, before it became too clogged (until now, I usually just waited until it was so clogged that it shut the engine down, but now I was trying to be proactive). I didn't want to face changing the filter while alone in a rolling sea. I was so sure I had it figured out this time... *don't forget the two valves on the fuel pump, and everything will be just fine.* I was thinking too far ahead. I forgot to fill the new filter with fuel before attaching it, and I subsequently ended up with so much air in the fuel lines, it was next to impossible to bleed the air out. After hours and hours of trying to bleed the air, I was frustrated to tears, literally. I started thinking that the ruins on the adjacent island would make a nice little fixer-upper, and that iguanas probably didn't taste *that* bad, as I tried to convince myself Allan's Cays would be an all right place to live out the rest of my days.

To bleed the air, it really is a two-person job to begin with, as the manual lever to pump the fuel is on one side, and the valves you need to wrench open are on the other. So, as you've likely come to expect by now, I eventually killed my batteries trying to start the engine. That's when fellow Canadians Wanda and Corstiaan came on the scene, saying they had a portable generator, and would be over in the morning to get the engine going.

It didn't take long the next day, and we didn't do anything different than I'd been doing the last few days. It was just a matter of getting every last microscopic air bubble out of the lines. So many people, when I mentioned I had a Perkins 4-108, would say, "Ah, right on. Great little engine!" I no longer agreed. How great is an engine, really, if you can *never* get it going after something as common as a filter change?

Corstiaan and Wanda loved to snorkel, and invited me along numerous times. We'd wait for near-slack tide and go to one of the cuts, then drift in the gentle current, as if viewing the coral, lobster, shells, and myriad of fish on a slide show. It was a fine anchorage to end my Bahamian tour.

Now that I had a working autopilot, I made the next segment of my journey an over-nighter. I decided I would head south of New Providence and up the Tongue of the Ocean, which would hopefully result in an early morning arrival at Northwest Channel, which was relatively narrow and I had no desire to face it in the dark.

I departed Allan's Cays at 8:00 AM and arrived at the southwestern tip of New Providence amidst a thunderstorm at dusk. There were thunderstorms encircling my position, from this point on, at any given moment, for the next three days. You could waste a lot of time and effort trying to steer around these storms, in the hopes of avoiding that *one* bolt of lightening that would take out all your electronics, or the high winds that could do other damage in many different ways. I decided to stay on my course, and for the first twenty-four hours this worked out very well. The distant (and not so distant) storms were essentially stationary, and just happened to not fall on my course line.

That first night, I managed two hours of sleep, motor-sailing in light and variable winds. I had an egg timer that I set in fifteen-minute increments. It worked well, though there was no way to mask the *tick-tick-tick-tick* as it counted down the minutes. I awoke from my last catnap an hour before sunrise, and felt surprisingly refreshed. By 9:30 AM, I was a couple of miles from the way-point I had entered in my hand-held GPS for Northwest Channel, and I watched as the harshest, blackest, most violent-looking squall line I had ever witnessed approached from dead ahead.

The Northwest Channel is essentially the end of the Tongue of the Ocean. The Tongue is wide and extremely deep, but as you approach the Channel, it gradually narrows, and, in the last quarter mile, shoals up from its average six-thousand-foot depths to less than twenty.

There were a few sport-fishing boats in the vicinity, and one large catamaran under full sail was going straight for the channel. He (or she) looked like they knew what they were doing, and I said to myself, *you get scared too easily, it's probably not as bad as it looks*. I made a decision to follow the catamaran. I thought the worst-case scenario would be a lot of wind and lightning and rain, but in that case, I could always drop my sails, motor through it, and let the autopilot do the work.

I had been thinking a lot lately, reflecting on my experiences thus far, the decisions I had made, what they had led to, and how many gut-wrenching situations I had found myself in, all with at least one other person aboard. I had been contemplating the inevitability of the day when I would find myself in a horrible situation, and only have myself to rely upon.

Today was to be that day.

I had dropped all my sails, but was still having serious second thoughts as I approached the channel. A wall of white suddenly enveloped the tall tower marking the edge of the reef, and the catamaran disappeared a few moments later. I felt sick to my stomach and was second-guessing my decision to follow the stranger, and without further ado, I put the boat on the opposite course to what I had been running. Too far to the right of that course, and I might hit the southern edge of the reef, too far to the left, and I might hit the northern edge. I really hadn't left myself very much sea room... how irresponsible. I had the feeling things were about to get bad, and I turned around to see what was coming, and not twenty feet off my stern were two waterspouts. I had seen plenty of waterspouts, fairly close when I was crewing on tall ships, and from afar on my own boat; but never *this* close, and never alone. My knees started to shake, and Effie looked frazzled as the sound of the spout hissed and salt water was being flung in our direction. I grabbed her and put her below, but she always hated being below with the sound of the engine running, so she promptly ran back on deck. I screamed at her at the top of my lungs, more out of fear for the general situation than for her not staying put, and grabbed her by the scruff of the neck and threw her below again, and then I jumped in behind her. I closed the hatch and doors, and looked out my window at the one waterspout that was still visible and just prayed it would stay where it was and not intensify. Then, the wind and lightning arrived.

The boat heeled over, and I felt her turn sharply, despite all sails being down, engine running, and the autopilot set for a course of 130 degrees. I did *not* want to go on deck. The lightning and thunder were simultaneous, and I was sure I'd be struck if I went up there. Looking at one of my many magnetic compasses I had down below, I could see I was pointed due north now. I felt trapped in a nightmare, you know the one; where someone is chasing you, and your limbs are made of lead, and you're trying to crawl away but your body won't obey your brain. I could not compute what was happening, my thoughts behaving like cold molasses. Where exactly am I? What are these sounds? Waterspouts, or just a solid wall of wind now? Can it really get *this* rough *this* quickly? North, north, what does that mean? I'm pointing north, why aren't I pointed southeast?

Then it hit me. North. Reef. To the north is reef!

I was already wearing my harness, the lanyard was on deck, wrapped around the mast, and ready to be clipped onto once I slid back the hatch. I crawled out, clipped in, jumped on the helm, and gave the engine a bit of throttle to keep ahead of the waves that *Annie Laurie* had already begun to surf. I thought I heard Effie once, assumed she was below, though I couldn't understand how I could possibly hear her if she was locked below, and with the wind screeching as loud as it was. I quickly forgot about her, and concentrated on my compass course, as it was very difficult to keep the boat going where I wanted her to go. With every lightening strike, I winced, expecting to be hit, or the boat to be hit, and I kept looking up to the top of the masts to search for damage after each strike, but the force of the rain pelting my eyeballs would have made any real attempt to see damage impossible. I don't want to exaggerate, so I'm going to estimate the winds at fifty knots, though I believe they were closer to sixty.

When I felt I had regained control of the boat, I took stock of the situation. I had dropped my GPS down below as I stumbled to grab it, and I couldn't leave the helm to go get it. Visibility was no more than fifty feet. I was surfing down closely spaced five to six foot waves, the rain was torrential, and the wind was no less persistent. The lightning seemed to be getting ahead of me, and I was breathing a tentative and silent sigh of relief in that regard. Other than not being able to determine my location, nothing else seemed of immediate danger.

I had never felt more alone in my entire life. I thought about how, if someone had been there with me, none of it would have seemed half as unnerving. As it was, the sound of the wind, the sight of the still-building seas and the occasional bolt of lightning seeped into my veins to produce a trauma that would take me *months* to entirely shrug off.

The storm lasted approximately one hour, and when it finally passed, I found myself nearly seven miles away from the channel. A storm petrel had landed on the foredeck and similarly appeared to be trying to shake itself of the experience, and its soaked feathers. This was my first chance to go look for Effie, who I'd spent the last agonizing hour fearing she had somehow been vacuumed overboard by a waterspout. I eventually found her in the chain locker at the bow, where she stayed for the next five or six hours, seeming more traumatized than I was. I brought offerings of tuna juice, in an attempt to apologize for what was out of my control.

She finally ventured into the main cabin late in the afternoon after spotting a small songbird that had flown below. I had been watching the bird for about ten minutes, after she had plopped out of the sky and onto my chart as I was attempting to plot a position. She had obviously been blown far from home (at this point I was over ten miles from the nearest shoreline). Effie tried to eat her, so I put her under a box on the deck hoping she would gain a bit of strength. I had unintentionally created an oven. She didn't make it.

That night, I had no option but to anchor on the banks. There was no land in sight, no protection, and the wind kept up at a steady twenty knots, which caused the boat to pitch and heave the entire night. Following the extreme stress of the earlier situation, my body was insisting I get some rest, but the weather wouldn't allow. And without sleep, even the smallest setbacks could abruptly reduce me to tears. I had spent *hours* at Allan's Cays devising and rigging a new bow roller, something to make hauling the anchor up by hand a little easier. It was ripped off my bowsprit by sunrise.

Two more days and I'll be safely in Miami.

The next evening I was anchored off Cat Cay. A small gap just north of the cay was the gateway to the final fifty miles to Miami. I crossed the reef at sunrise, setting a way-point for twenty miles south of Miami, anticipating the distance the Gulf Stream would set me off my intended course. It worked out perfectly. I arrived just east of Fowey Rocks outside of Miami at sunset. By mid-afternoon, I knew I was going to be crossing the reef after sunset, and just hoped the cloud cover would dissipate so the moon would at least make certain landmarks easier to see and navigate by. Having been in the sparsely inhabited Bahamas for four months, I had forgotten about the notion of light pollution, and so I need not have worried about having sufficient light around a city as large as Miami.

At 10:00 PM I was safely at anchor in No Name Harbour, a comfortable anchorage I had visited a couple of times before. What a tremendous relief. I felt my trials of recent days had finally come to an end.

I didn't yet know I was about to encounter weather odds that I'd rather *not* have beaten.

Twenty- One

The chance of a boat being struck by lightning in the United States is 1.2 in 1000. In Florida, that statistic becomes 4 in 1000.

I hadn't been in Miami two days before the storm hit, and as far as electrical storms went, this one fell under the category of severe. A constant barrage of lightning was reaching the surface throughout the anchorage, and from the beginning, I felt it was inevitable that I'd be struck. I hoped my lightning-rod system would do its job properly. The tops of the masts are metal, the stays supporting them are metal, and are attached to the wooden hull by metal plates. The keel bolts are big rods of stainless steel, so with a thick copper wire bridging the gap from the metal plates to the keel bolts, the boat should have been grounded to the surrounding ocean. The rolling low clouds had the appearance of dirty thick smoke from a nearby inferno, grabbed and hurled eastward by raging upper-level winds. When the lightning hit, it lasted for two or three seconds, to the best of my memory. There was a *pop,* which was soon followed by the smell of burning. It smelled metallic, not wooden, but on instinct, I ran on deck in the midst of the storm to double-check that I didn't have an impending disaster on my hands. Convinced all was well for the moment, I went below, grabbed my softest blanket and curled up helpless on the bunk, waiting for the remainder of the storm to pass.

The calm sunset that followed seemed like nature's defiance, pretending nothing had happened at all. As I wandered around the deck, a melted VHF antenna was the most obvious of the clues. The lack of response when turning on various electronics confirmed what I feared. My newly working autopilot and depth sounder were fried. *Annie Laurie* was traditional through and through, and nature assisted her in rejecting any new technology that might make navigating and journeying easier or more pleasurable. Much like her owner, she seemed prone to doing things the hard way.

That was early June, and what drew me to Miami in the first place kept me there for six weeks. As he had promised when we met in the Exumas, should I ever visit him in Miami, Phil showed me some of the finer things Miami had to offer. I had been there twice before, anchoring in the area for a few weeks combined, but had never been ashore. I'm sometimes a quick judge of character, and I decided the city was full of rogues and thieves; and guns, lots of guns. While that probably remained true to a certain point, there's certainly a lot more to the city.

Phil took me to botanical gardens, full of hundreds of tropical trees, plants and flowers, and could very well be the world headquarters for mosquito production. He demonstrated how to drive defensively in Miami, the city deemed to have the country's most dangerous drivers in North America (five years running), and he showed me the joys of riding a motorcycle. We toured around the neighbourhood he grew up in, on the fringes of the city, surrounded by tropical tree farms, fruit stands, and fields of strawberries and mango trees. We explored the trendy South Beach area by bicycle, and watched the busy shipping activity from the Port of Miami.

As you could expect, making the decision to leave Miami was one I struggled with. It was time to get *Annie Laurie* out of the hot southern waters, her wooden hull being sensitive to the extreme heat and humidity, and local teredo worms. I knew her return to Lunenburg needed to happen sooner rather than later. I had about 1700 miles of ocean to traverse between Miami and home. Now I felt in a rush to get there, and knew very well that if I had to hop my way slowly up the coast (as I would have to do without crew or autopilot), that it would take me months, rather than weeks.

With the help of a friendly, displaced Irishman named Gerry, I had a replacement depth-sounder in hand. I sent my autopilot off for repair, and put out a call for crew. I had a lot of feedback, but in the end, only one person came through. My Dad flew to Miami one evening, and having my refurbished autopilot back in place, we left the following morning from the Miami River, winding our way past the construction and skyscrapers and dockyards, bound for the Atlantic.

I remember looking back one last time before we rounded the bend in the river, to see Phil standing on the stern of *Retriever*, wondering when we'd see each other again. At this point I had no other choice but to look ahead and face the task at hand; about 750 miles of open ocean to North Carolina with my Dad, who had never been to sea.

§§§

It hadn't really occurred to me that Dad might require some tips on boat handling. As soon as we cleared Government Cut and I was relatively comfortable that we were far enough off Miami Beach, I went below to make breakfast. The only instruction I left Dad was to hang a left and run parallel to the beach after the next red buoy.

We were motoring, as there was little wind on this hot, sunny summer day. When the engine was running and you were down below, it was difficult to hear anything that might be going on above deck. I was too preoccupied with bagels and eggs to realize that Dad was trying to inform me that both the steering and compass had spontaneously stopped working as soon as I handed him the helm.

"The compass keeps spinning in circles, and I'm turning the wheel further and we keep going the wrong way." We had circumnavigated the red buoy, and were once again inbound towards Miami. This trip was going to be a learning experience for both of us.

We had roughly set our sights on Beaufort, North Carolina as our next port. The first forty-eight hours in the Gulf Stream were very encouraging. Making nine knots over the ground at the time, it seemed like it might be a very short trip. That first night was our last sight of Florida, as the distant lights of West Palm Beach faded with the morning light. From here, we'd be going out of our way if we were to follow the coast.

Every few hours, distant threatening thunderclouds would form, and the gut-wrenching alarmist warnings on the VHF would only make matters worse, instilling feelings of dread and panic. The electronic voice seemed to imply that it was completely unreasonable to be making such a passage this time of year offshore, when frequent storms were inevitable, and impending doom was almost certain. But fortunately for us the storms stayed at bay, and cheerfully, we sailed onward.

Our first sight to make the empty sea seem less lonely was a NASA commissioned ship, out to recover the booster rockets from a launch at Cape Canaveral two nights earlier. I hailed them over the VHF for an update on the tropical cyclone probability, as we were now out of range of the regular shore-based broadcasts, and last I'd heard there was a high probability of tropical storm development with a particular area of low pressure in the eastern Caribbean. If development had continued, I was considering ducking back towards the mainland, and possibly pulling into Charleston to hide from the weather if necessary. The officer aboard the ship informed me that the low had dissipated, and so we continued to aim for North Carolina.

As the second night fell upon us, the skies were crystal clear and the wind was steady, pushing us along at a comfortable six knots, as we continued to get a bit of help from the Gulf Stream. The wind continued to build as midnight approached, and though I'm sure it never exceeded twenty-five knots, I became increasingly on edge. The seas were confused without explanation, which added to my feeling of unease. It was still hot, so Dad and I both stayed on deck as the autopilot did the work. As I laid down snuggling into my flannel pillowcase and a micro-fleece blanket Phil had sent along for the trip, I thought about how great it was that my little boat was such a 'dry' boat (no matter what the sea conditions, the cockpit generally stayed dry). So naturally, moments later, I was drenched and choking on a load of warm seawater. My new favourite blanket and only tangible reminder of Phil would now be slimy and salty for the next four days and would not be there for my comfort.

Aside from being soaked, the incident left me with the feeling that something worse was on the way. The winds were already fifteen knots higher than forecast, and I had a million things running through my head. After the 'rogue' wave, Dad had retreated below to avoid a soaking in the case of a repeat performance. He popped his head up for a second and asked something along the lines of "Is this normal?" to which I said, "Yeah, This is nothing..." He believed me, and it was in fact a true statement, though I really didn't feel that way at the time. I tend to lose the nerve required to be at sea in a small boat when I spend too much time living the easy life ashore, as I'd done for close to six weeks in Miami.

Aside from the NASA ship, the sea was completely devoid of traffic until 4:00 AM on day four, when *both* Dad and I had inadvertently fallen asleep on deck, and he awoke first to see a city of lights just off our starboard quarter. He jumped up and quite innocently asked, "What is that?" It took me a few seconds to process what was happening. Every single deck light aboard this cargo ship was brightly lit; it looked like a city skyline. I couldn't find a red or green light amongst the sea of lights to indicate the direction in which the ship was travelling. I figured one of the hundred white lights I could see was a stern light, and the ship was moving away. But as my eyes came into better focus I could see the ship's green light, indicating they were moving across our stern, meaning we had just cut in front of them. We had just completed a game of chicken with a very large ship that was probably never aware we existed. This was exactly why I hadn't wanted to do this trip alone, so we wouldn't overlook the two-hundred-foot ships bound for Charleston. It happened anyway, but we were lucky.

To nicely round out the first leg of our journey, a pod of dolphins came to visit and play on our last afternoon at sea. I was glad to see how much Dad was enjoying the experience, as I myself had begun to take such incidences in stride. It's a bit sad to realize that you can come to view such an enchanting event as ordinary.

The toughest challenge of this part of the trip was actually the entry into the harbour at Beaufort, North Carolina. True to my cruising style, I had scribbled down a way-point from online charts that would get me to the outer approaches of the channel, then I had a sketch from a cruising guide that made the entrance look fairly straight-forward; red, green, red, green, hang a left, hang a right, drop the hook, pop the cork on that last bottle of wine.

My first regret was that we would be arriving after dark. My second regret was the four-knot tidal current running at its peak. My third regret was the two outbound tugboats coming around the corner towing an unlit barge, in an area where shoaling requires frequent dredging and the danger of running aground is ever-present. My final regret was not having the proper detailed chart. The red and green lights marking a winding path were all flashing different patterns, clues to which ones to aim for first (if I had the chart to break the code). All I could think of, as I was made dizzy by the flashing lights, was the lights of Phil's pinball machine. It's a less exciting game when your boat is the ball, large steel buoys and barges and tugboats and sandbars are the pins, and a strong current is trying its best to force you into a collision with at least one of them.

I found the pressure a bit intense as I struggled to figure out where we were, and constantly feared we were on the verge of hitting bottom. My brain managed to organize all the lights into two possible channels, but I was at a loss as to which one I should follow. I looked up, and no joke, a shooting star streamed directly down one of the two perceived channels. It's a good thing I believe in signs.

By 1:00 AM we were finally in the crowded anchorage, and I was fumbling to get my computer on deck to scavenge a wireless signal to talk to Phil for the first time in what felt like a century.

§§§

For the next few days, we would have it relatively easy. We were heading up the Intracoastal Waterway to Norfolk, Virginia, so we would be motoring from mark to mark, and we could anchor somewhere every night for a good nights sleep. The only fear I constantly harboured, which would have been the same had we been out on the open ocean, was the frequent summertime thunderstorms. The only downside of being in the constricted waterways was if a storm struck, I had little choice but to stay on deck and steer through it, to ensure we wouldn't be blown aground. At sea, I could run below and we could drift as we waited for the storm to pass.

At the end of day three on the ICW, we arrived in Portsmouth, Virginia, where we waited for a three to four day weather window to sail directly to Cape Cod. We had managed to make it from Beaufort to the Chesapeake Bay unscathed by thunderstorms, but this wouldn't be true for the next leg of the trip.

The next four days were miserable. The

autopilot kicked the bucket once again as we left Portsmouth, so one of us would always have to be at the helm. The water, and therefore the air temperature, got progressively colder, and there were frequent squalls, whose winds always seemed to oppose the prevailing winds, which made for sloppy seas. We were getting slammed around in a very unsteady and unpredictable manner, which caused me great anxiety, for no matter what I've put the boat through in the past, and how many times she's proven herself, in the back of my mind I'm always thinking *maybe today's the day she'll spring a plank*. Of course, she never did, but I always feared that if I stopped worrying about it, that is when it would finally happen. I've noticed this aspect of my character in many situations. My favourite words of reassurance have become those of Sir Winston Churchill, roughly along the lines of 'I've had many worries in my lifetime, most of which never happened.' How often do we abandon moments of peaceful happiness as we worry about things that will likely never come to pass?

The sea had been empty since a Navy destroyer in the approaches of the Chesapeake Bay overtook us. We were three days along and I calculated our arrival in Quissett Harbour to be the following afternoon. We were as far from shore as we would be for this part of the trip, about 130 miles from Long Island, and another black squall line with vicious lightning was fast approaching, and there was no place to hide. I had resolved to run below as the squall reached us, but as luck would have it, a long-liner appeared out of the mist and was on a path to cross my bow. I sent Dad below and crouched in the cockpit (like that might somehow have dampened the impact of a lightning strike) and steered around the fishing boat and its trailing gear as the storm passed. Once safe, I called down to reassure Dad the worst was over. Apparently he wasn't terribly concerned; he was sound asleep.

After that squall, the sky turned an unnerving shade of grey, and for a while the winds increased to thirty knots, and whitecaps were appearing on the larger swells. Just eighteen more hours, and we'd be in the safety of Buzzards Bay, west of Cape Cod. So anxious to get there, I decided to haul the sails in tight and motor sail the rest of the way. In the rough seas, I realized it would only be a matter of time before the remaining crud in the bottom of the fuel tank would be stirred up and would clog the filters, eventually shutting down the engine. I hoped beyond all hope that it would last us until Quissett Harbour.

It was around 2:00 AM when that old familiar racing sound of the fuel-deprived engine began. My autopilot had stopped working again, so I had to wake Dad to come steer while I went to replace the filter. Unfortunately, replacing the secondary filter did not fix the problem. I once again faced bleeding the fuel lines after replacing the primary filter, which, if you've been paying close attention, I have *never* managed to do without killing the starter battery and eventually relying on outside help (shore power or borrowed generators, and at least one more person to press the manual fuel pump on one side of the engine while I cracked the various fuel lines on the other side). This would be my first attempt of this at sea. If I was unsuccessful, it could mean a very slow slog the rest of the way to Cape Cod under sail power alone, and in the current weather conditions, this could take *days*.

I was very careful to do every step correctly the first time. I had never had to do this in rough seas in the middle of the night before, and as sleep-deprived as I was, I didn't have much faith in myself. Once finished, I clenched my hands together as Dad turned the ignition key, and to my amazement, it started immediately. First time *ever*, with my own two hands and no outside help. I felt I had finally conquered the last demon residing in my engine. So, four hours later, when it happened again, I had a lot more confidence. By the *third* time (give me a break!) I was becoming competitive with myself, and now it was all about speed. I knew I could do it; I just wanted to break my previous record.

We sailed into the lee of Elizabeth Island, Cape Cod, just as the weather was becoming really lousy. I don't know how much longer I could have watched the waves build higher and higher from behind. I'd been traumatized one too many times in recent months, and now anything but ideal conditions left me praying for safe harbour. As we drifted into smoother waters, a thick fog settled in. Aside from the possibility of other boat traffic, I wasn't terribly worried about the declining visibility because, for once, I had charts for these waters.

Once inside Quissett Harbour, the sun broke through and the fog evaporated. We picked up a mooring, and a wireless signal, and were able to make contact with Ben from *The Eye*, who had moved to Cape Cod since I'd last seen him at the Great Bridge Lock almost two years earlier.

Once again, Ben and Brigid opened up their new home to us, and we had a great time catching up on each other's lives. We played on Ben's homemade Parcheesi board and enjoyed great barbeque dinners over bottles of wine. Ben helped with various boat issues, arranging a mooring for us close to the dinghy dock; fuel, fresh water, and he determined the solution for the most recent problem with the autopilot. Before leaving, I thought it would be prudent to change the fuel filter one more time, while in a calm harbour, sitting still on the mooring. I did, and do you think I could get that engine started afterwards? After a frustrating couple of hours, it was Ben to the rescue.

Ben came aboard as we departed for a final

goodbye, before taking to his dinghy and casting off. We set our course for the nearby Cape Cod Canal.

I timed the tides correctly this time for heading east through the canal. Once through, we had a beautiful sail across Cape Cod Bay to Provincetown. From here, it would be only three more days to the anchorage in Lunenburg Harbour.

We were almost home.

Twenty-Two

The three-day passage from Provincetown to Nova Scotia was bitterly cold, but it got off to a great start. We were just a couple of hours out of Cape Cod when we came within a few meters of a couple of massive whales, who were determined to stay by our side for a while. Shortly after, a thick fog rolled in, and our next glimpse of land was the rock breakwater in Lunenburg.

Rowing ashore one last time in Lunenburg, I looked back at *Annie Laurie* not knowing if the next time I saw her she would still be mine. I had a flight to catch shortly that would take me to Newfoundland for another forecasting contract. I had resigned myself to the fact that she had to go up for sale, considering many of my current personal circumstances. Of course I cried.

I was feeling a bit shell-shocked upon arriving in St John's mid-August. It would be a huge change after the freedom of living on a boat for the past three years. I did an excellent job of not allowing myself to become attached to any part of Newfoundland life. I would occasionally visit the pub or attend parties with coworkers, but I would always get home early for my nightly phone call from Phil. It seemed like an impossible situation to resolve, yet my hopes were high during those first few months apart. I had no doubt where things were leading, and that somehow, somewhere, we'd see each other again.

And so in October, Phil made his first trip to Canada. I took him to places that I thought would impress him, but like a kid who gets everything for Christmas and tosses it all aside to make a fort out of the cardboard boxes, what I really remember was his fascination with the massive pile of road salt (not a common sight in Miami) on the waterfront that had been offloaded from a ship a few days earlier. Forget Signal Hill or Cape Spear, he wanted his photo taken next to the giant mountain of salt.

We crammed three holidays into the ten-day visit, knowing we wouldn't be together for Halloween, (American) Thanksgiving, or Christmas. We carved pumpkins and went into the forest for a small Christmas tree, which we decorated and placed on top of the Franklin fireplace in my apartment. We tried fried cod tongues for the first time, deciding Newfoundlanders must have been desperate for sustenance when first sampling the dish.

A month later, I flew to Miami to spend New Years with him. We had now spent a grand total of one month together, but it didn't even take that long to know where we wanted things to go. We knew at first sight in the Bahamas. Now we were left to figure out how to remove the 2000 miles between us.

All the while, *Annie Laurie* was sitting outside Lunenburg awaiting a couple of repairs, and a potential buyer. I just couldn't see how she fit into my future, though I felt like a bad mother, abandoning her child when it became the slightest bit inconvenient. But, I reasoned, you have to leave certain things behind to open yourself up to new experiences. I had a pretty good run with *Annie Laurie,* and perhaps I had already accomplished everything I was meant to do with her.

The memories, though, were painful. I longed to be aboard again, and to relive so much of what I had been through. Some days I had to block the memories completely, because it was too much to take, thinking back to the extraordinarily good times, and now feeling so lost and alone in the cold and bitter darkness of winter in Newfoundland.

Annie Laurie would not be forgotten though. One evening before heading to bed, I had a message in my inbox, with the subject heading *Message in the Bottle*. It had been nine months since I had thrown the messages-in-wine-bottles into the Gulf Stream on my way to the Bahamas.

The message read:

Dear Laura,

I'm Cláudia. I'm writing for you because my cousin found your letter in the bottle. He found it yesterday, Sunday, when he is fishing. Your letter, sailing in the sea during 9 months and became to Terceira Island, in Azores, Portugal. I like your story very much and I think is important you know where your message come. And I believe that with little steps we can change the world. Good luck for you and your adventures and I hope that you enjoy your opportunities along the way.
Your friend in middle of Atlantic,
Cláudia

The third Monday in January, known as Blue Monday, is, statistically speaking, the most depressing day of the year. That January in particular I had no problem believing it to be true. By January 18th, I'd grown weary, losing the hope and resilience required to follow what my heart had chosen months before. *Annie Laurie* was reluctantly for sale in Nova Scotia, and I started asking myself how often long-distance relationships realistically work out. Was it really any more than a fling? Something genuine between two people feeling a mutual attraction, but never meaning to go beyond the few good times we'd already

248

experienced? Who wouldn't romanticize the events of a few precious seedling memories in the far-away tropics, good as they were, but made even better when juxtaposed with the St. John's winter?

Once again, I was making use of my education, unhappy in my "great" job, wondering if it was true this day had always been inevitable; the day I would rejoin the *real world*. I'd had my turn at adventure and freedom, and now it was time to be guilted into the responsible life that everyone, if life is to be fair, is required to follow.

Can we live our lives by doing what feels right in the moment? Can we trust that things will fall into place before we see the big picture? If we choose to fulfill the expectations of family, friends, and society, with all their good, if not misguided, intentions, can we be any more certain of what our futures have in store, or that it would ultimately be for the best?

I was in a most desperate state of limbo. Then, late one night, as I sat waiting to send out my midnight forecasts, the phone rang. It was Phil, proposing a plan that involved us never having to say goodbye to each other again.